THE KEY TO
LASTING
JOY

FOREWORD BY
BILLY GRAHAM

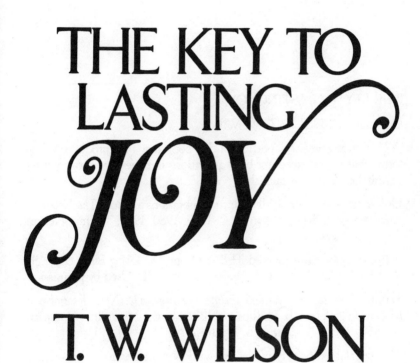

THE KEY TO
LASTING
JOY

T. W. WILSON

WORD BOOKS
PUBLISHER
WACO, TEXAS

A DIVISION OF
WORD, INCORPORATED

Library of Congress Cataloging-in-Publication Data

Wilson, T. W., 1918-
  The key to lasting joy.

  1. Christian life—Baptist authors. I. Title.
BV4501.2.W5635 1987   248.4   87-2117

Printed in the United States of America.

CONTENTS

FOREWORD

Dr. T. W. Wilson has been one of my closest friends and associates throughout my ministry—and even before! His face is usually beaming and almost always he exhibits the joy of the Lord. He has now written a book entitled *The Key to Lasting Joy.* In it, he asks the question: *Why do so many people go through life searching for happiness and joy—yet never finding it?*

In this book "T," as we affectionately call him, correctly affirms that joy is not something we can manufacture by our own strength. Nor is it something which comes to us only when our circumstances are ideal. It is instead a fruit of the Spirit which God gives us when we serve Him—and a gift God desires to bestow on every believer. And it comes not as we pursue it as an end in itself, but as we submit ourselves to Christ and actively serve Him daily through our lives and our witness. Joy through serving Christ—that's the key to lasting satisfaction and peace for every believer!

"T" is constantly reading his Bible and has a wealth of knowledge from his personal walk with God and his work for the Lord in many parts of the world. Out of his study and experience he examines why there is so little joy in our lives. His emphasis on complete submission to Christ and the necessity for moral purity is greatly needed today. He also shows how God can work through a variety of people and methods. His challenge for Christians to be on the evangelistic cutting edge of God's work needs to be heard and heeded by every believer in the world.

The Key to Lasting Joy could change your life! I do not know a greater need today than for the people who claim to be followers of Christ to totally commit themselves—whether it is to Christ's call of discipleship—or our marriage vows. In every area of our lives we are to be totally surrendered. When we are, we can be filled with the Holy Spirit, Who will supernaturally produce the fruit of the Spirit in us (of which joy is one of the nine components listed in Galatians 5).

I heartily commend and recommend this book. It is my prayer that God will use it in a unique way to point many to Christ and challenge believers everywhere to be faithful disciples so that the world may know something of the grace, mercy, and forgiveness of God—and the tremendous change He can bring in anyone's life who is willing to be committed to Him.

BILLY GRAHAM

PREFACE

This book was born out of my personal experiences and preaching over many years. I have delivered the basic content of this book to several schools of evangelism during various Billy Graham crusades. Over the years, God has burdened my heart with the absolute necessity of proclaiming His holy Word and making His living Word relevant to humanity's needs in today's world. In this book, therefore, I tried to face some of the great issues confronting the church today, while also making the explanation of God's truths appropriate for those who may be new Christians.

I want to give special thanks to Larry Weeden for his help in writing *The Key to Lasting Joy*. He took my thoughts and my words and made a finished book out of them. Also, I owe a lasting debt of gratitude to Larry Stone for editing *The Key to Lasting Joy* and for giving excellent guidance along the way.

My wife and companion of forty-four years, Mary Helen, has made the entire project possible. Had it not been for her cooperation, love, and encouragement, I would not have been able to do my evangelistic work. She has been my most loyal and trusted advisor.

T. W. WILSON

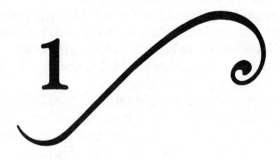

THE KEY TO
LASTING JOY

TO ALL OUTWARD APPEARANCES, Hank and Sam and the lives they lead are very much alike. Appearances can be deceiving, however, for there are important differences between Hank and Sam, and those differences make a tremendous impact on the quality of their lives.

Hank and Sam are about the same age. They're both happily married and have children whom they love. Their salaries and standards of living are roughly equivalent; like most of us, they sometimes run out of money before the end of the month, but they dress well, eat well, and have comfortable homes and cars.

The two of them also belong to the same church, and here again their lives seem very similar. Both they and their families are very active. They attend worship services and Sunday school faithfully. They serve on various committees, they help with fellowship dinners, and they can be counted on to support the church program in whatever way is needed. Hank teaches a Sunday school class, and Sam often helps out with the youth group. If you asked others in the church, including the pastor, what they think of Hank and Sam, they would describe them both as solid, valuable members of the congregation.

People in the community would also say that Hank and Sam are very much alike. Hank and Sam keep up their yards and homes, and they get along well with their neighbors. They also volunteer their time and effort to charitable causes. Hank, for example, is active in the PTA. Sam takes part in the annual cancer fund drive.

Yes, to all outward appearances, Sam and Hank are very similar men leading good, middle-class lives that are much alike.

But looking just at those outward appearances doesn't begin to tell us the whole story of their lives. In reality, Hank is a happy, joyful, and fulfilled person who believes his life is important. He is content with the lot in life that God has given him, and he is convinced that as God works through him he is making a real contribution of lasting value to the world.

Sam, however, when he is honest with himself and his closest friends, admits that he often feels dissatisfied, discontented, and downright miserable. He has no lasting joy. He doesn't like his job, his house, his role in the church, or the general direction of his life. And worst of all, he feels his life is a waste, even though there are so many demands on his time that he seems to live in a constant state of exhaustion.

What are some of the other important differences between Hank and Sam? For one thing, Hank has a very clear sense of what God wants of him and the way he uses his time, energy, and money. Sam, on the other hand, does not have that sense of direction. Most of the time he's working hard to accumulate possessions. When he does think about his Christian life, he envisions the saintly pastor of their church and tries to figure out how he could be just like him.

For another thing, Sam has a few areas of his life that he doesn't let anyone else know about, areas where he indulges in thoughts and behavior that he knows the Bible calls sin. Sure, he feels an occasional twinge of guilt about cheating on his income tax return every year, for example, but he rationalizes away those feelings by saying to himself that everyone else does it, too. And besides, the government already takes too much of his hard-earned money.

In contrast, Hank is trying to lead a life pleasing to God in every way. He fails from time to time, and he struggles in some areas more than others. He's got quite a temper, for one thing, and he occasionally gets angry with a person for the wrong reasons. But rather than ignore or try to hide his sins, he confesses them to God, knowing He forgives. Hank is then able to get on with his life with a clean conscience and in close fellowship with his heavenly Father.

Another difference is that Hank speaks out boldly when he sees a need and feels God is calling him to be involved. When Sam sees a similar need, he lacks the courage to take a stand. This difference showed up recently when a bookstore selling pornographic materials opened for business near the school Hank's and Sam's children attend. Hank was deeply concerned about the influence of such a store on the school children, and also about the kind of customers the store would attract so close to the school.

He took his concern to the school's PTA and led it in petitioning the police to enforce the local zoning ordinances against a business of that sort being so close to the school. In a couple of months, the store was forced to move to a location away from any schools.

Sam saw what was happening, agreed with what Hank was doing, and greatly admired Hank for caring enough to get involved. But Sam was "too busy" to take part himself. And besides, there were already enough people working on it to get the job done.

Finally, Hank is deeply committed to the work of evangelization, and it gives a purpose to his life that makes every day an
exciting challenge. Now, he's never thought he was supposed to
go to Africa as a missionary, and he's not unusually aggressive
about personal soul winning. But he supports several missionary
families with both his money and his prayers, and when people
ask him what makes him different, he's not shy about discussing
what Christ means in his life.

Sam, on the other hand, has never seen anything appealing
about missions. He'd just as soon see the money he gives to the
church go toward beautifying the sanctuary. And when it comes to
talking about spiritual things, he'd prefer that his non-Christian
friends didn't even know about his faith. After all, he doesn't want
them to think he's weird!

The Crucial Difference

All these differences between the satisfied, fulfilled Hank and
the unhappy, frustrated Sam grow out of one crucial difference
that is central to their lives. At the core of his being, Hank has
chosen to be a servant of Jesus Christ. And that crucial difference
is the key to lasting joy. Day by day, moment by moment, Hank
doesn't seek his own will or his own advantage, but he seeks to
live the way he believes Christ would want him to live. He's not
perfect by any means, and because he knows that, he's one of the
most humble people you'll ever meet. If you asked people who
know him to describe him in a word, you'd hear things like "joy,"
"purpose," "strength," and "love."

Sam also has heard about what it means to be a servant, and he
has the example of people like Hank. But he's never been willing
to give complete control of his life over to Christ. He's afraid that
doing that would take all the pleasure out of life, although he'll
never say so publicly, and he really believes that a little more
money, a nicer and newer car, and a bigger house are all he needs
to be happy in life.

Now, lest you judge Sam too quickly or label him a fool, let's be
honest and confess that many Christians are at least a little bit like

him. And many more are exactly like him—or worse. They just can't buy the idea that being a servant to *anybody* could mean anything but loss of freedom and pure drudgery.

Both Hank and Sam want lasting joy. And I'm sure you do too. Jesus Christ said that He came to bring it to you when He said, "I have come that they may have life, and that they may have it more abundantly" (John 10:10). But many of us—like Sam—think that lasting joy comes from more money, a nicer car, a bigger house, perhaps a new husband or wife. The truth is, *those things will not bring lasting joy.*

The book of Proverbs pictures two paths for a person to follow: the way of wisdom and the way of folly. In some parts of the book, following these two paths are graphically portrayed as rejoicing "with the wife of your youth" (5:18) or following after "an immoral woman" (5:3). The difference between the two is not in what they promise—both wisdom and folly promise joy. The difference is in which one lastingly fulfills the promise. The key to lasting joy is not in following the way of folly (the "immoral woman"), no matter how attractive or seductive it may be.

There is no more reliable truth I could tell you than that the key to lasting joy is to be a servant of the Lord Jesus Christ. It is the most rewarding and satisfying life possible. When you choose to be a servant, you don't lose, I assure you. You win! You *will* have lasting joy.

Perhaps you have been a Christian for many years, yet—like Sam—you are dissatisfied and unfulfilled. Perhaps you have just become a Christian and want to know more about serving the God Who has saved you. Perhaps you are not yet a Christian, but want to know more about the Christian life. I urge you to read on, for in these pages you will find how to live a life that will bring you lasting joy.

I have had the pleasure of serving Billy Graham for many years. It is a privilege and one of the most demanding jobs I can imagine. But more than that, I am a servant of Jesus Christ, and that relationship for which I volunteered is the key to my life. As I have traveled the world with Billy, I have seen over and over the basic truth that I want to convey very clearly to you in this book: Those who give themselves as servants of God have the thrill of being a part of what He's doing in this world; those who will not be servants are at heart dissatisfied with life, and when they're in the church they hinder its work. Being a servant of God is the key to the lasting joy we all desire.

In the chapters that follow, I want to show you exactly what it means to be God's servant. There are four major facets to this life, and I'll develop each one carefully so you can understand them clearly. Jesus urged us to count the cost before we commit ourselves to anything important (see Luke 14:28–30), and that advice is as wise today as ever. I will show you that the life of a servant of God is no perpetual bed of roses. But I will also demonstrate that *it is far more exciting, satisfying, and joyful than any other life you can choose.*

If you know your life isn't all it could be, if you want to have lasting joy, if you see more of yourself in my description of Sam than in my account of Hank, read on. My prayer is that you will accept the challenge of being nothing less than all God intends for you, that you will accept for yourself the truth that the most exciting journey in the world begins by bowing your knee before your Savior and Lord.

Part I

A CLEAR
CALL

WHAT IS A
SERVANT?

ONCE UPON A TIME, there was a frog who wanted to live like a prince. He dreamed of representing the king as an ambassador to foreign nations. Or perhaps he could be a general in the king's army and conquer his master's enemies. Most of all, he craved the friendship and trust of the king. He yearned to sit beside the throne and discuss important affairs of state with the monarch, serving the king with his wise counsel.

There was just one problem with this marvelous dream. The frog was a frog who lived in a swamp, not a prince in a palace. He couldn't live like a prince because he wasn't a prince—he was about as far from it as it was possible to be. In order for him to live like a prince, there would first have to be a total, miraculous transformation in his life. He would have to become something entirely different. He would have to become a prince.

Unfortunately for the frog, as you and I know, such wonderful changes of fortune are only the stuff of which fairy tales are made. Real life for frogs will always mean living in swamps and eating insects.

The story of the human race is very much like that of the frog, only for us there is a great deal more hope.

In its sinfulness, humanity naturally lives far removed from the presence of God the Sovereign. People swim in a swamp of envy, lust, and hatred. Like our frog, however, we yearn for far more—for fellowship with the King, for life in His glorious presence, for meaningful joy-filled purpose to our existence. And like the frog, we would need to be totally transformed into something entirely new—princes and princesses—before that could be possible.

Now here's the exciting news. Whereas frogs become princes only in fairy tales, we can in real life become children of God! In fact, that's exactly what God wants, and He's done everything to make it possible.

This is a book about lasting joy, and the first chapter was written to show you that the key to lasting joy is to become a servant of Jesus Christ, which is the most satisfying and fulfilling life possible. Now I want to show you exactly what it means to be His servant, and the first and most important truth is that we have to be transformed. We have to shed these frog bodies and become princes and princesses. We must become part of His family because He gives lasting joy only to His own children.

Servants Are First Children

How do we become part of God's family? We go through a process that's simple to understand and yet life-changing. Jesus called it being "born again" (see John 3:3–7).

We begin by acknowledging before God that we fall far short of His holiness. The Bible tells us, "For all have sinned and fall short of the glory of God" (Rom. 3:23). Again it says, "There is none righteous, no, not one" (Rom 3:10). The prophet Isaiah put it like this: "All we like sheep have gone astray; we have turned, every one, to his own way" (53:6).

Having confessed to God that we are sinners deserving His judgment, we recognize and believe by faith that God, in love, has provided the way for us to be reconciled to Himself. He did this through the life, death, and resurrection of His Son, our Lord Jesus Christ. "But God demonstrates His own love toward us, in that while we were still sinners, Christ died for us" (Rom. 5:8). We also read, "For the wages of sin is death, but the gift of God is eternal life in Christ Jesus our Lord" (Rom. 6:23).

Two of the most beautiful passages in Scripture, both penned by the apostle John, speak further to this crucial issue. As 1 John 4:9–10 says, "In this the love of God was manifested toward us, that God has sent His only begotten Son into the world, that we might live through Him. In this is love, not that we loved God, but that He loved us and sent His Son to be the propitiation [satisfactory payment] for our sins."

And John 3:16 tells us, "For God so loved the world that He gave His only begotten Son, that whoever believes in Him should not perish but have everlasting life."

Unlike every other human being who has ever lived, Jesus Christ led a perfect, sinless life. Then, He allowed Himself to be nailed to a Roman cross so that He could take upon Himself the guilt of our sins and pay the price we owed to a righteous God. It is because Christ's sacrifice on our behalf satisfied the justice of God that we can be restored to fellowship with Him. As the apostle Paul said in 2 Corinthians 5:21, "He [the Father] made Him who knew no sin [Jesus] to be sin for us, that we might become the righteousness of God in Him."

If we have understood and believed what Christ has done to make our peace with God possible, how do we appropriate it for ourselves and know that we personally are God's children? Again, God's Word tells us: "Whoever calls upon the name of the Lord [Jesus] shall be saved" (Rom. 10:13). "But as many as received Him [Jesus], to them He gave the right to become children of God, even to those who believe in His name" (John 1:12). "If you confess with your mouth the Lord Jesus and believe in your heart that God has raised Him from the dead, you will be saved. For with the heart one believes to righteousness, and with the mouth confession is made to salvation" (Rom. 10:9–10).

Remember that Romans 6:23 describes eternal life as a gift. And as with any gift, you have to accept it. By faith you have to say, "I believe Jesus died and rose for me, to pay for my sins. I accept His gift of life and submit myself to His lordship."

Let me put this in the context of servanthood again. Naturally, a faithful servant wants to please his master. Now, how do we please God best if we would serve Him? We obey His commands and do His work. The apostle John told us, "This is His commandment: that we should believe on the name of His Son Jesus Christ" (1 John 3:23). Jesus said, "This is the work of God, that you believe in Him whom He sent" (John 6:29).

If you have never confessed your sin to God, believed that His Son, Jesus, is the only way of salvation, and received Him as your Savior and Lord, committing your life to Him, I urge you to do so now. Don't delay. Don't let anything keep you from making this most crucial decision of your life.

Once you have made this decision, placing yourself by faith in the hands of God, you have the marvelous assurance of God's Word that you are His forever. Jesus said of those who believe in Him, "I give them eternal life, and they shall never perish; neither shall anyone snatch them out of My hand. My Father, who has given them to Me, is greater than all; and no one is able to snatch them out of My Father's hand" (John 10:28–29).

The apostle John underlines that promise: "And this is the testimony: that God has given us eternal life, and this life is in His Son. He who has the Son has life; he who does not have the Son of God does not have life. These things I have written to you who believe in the name of the Son of God, that you may know that you have eternal life, and that you may continue to believe in the name of the Son of God" (1 John 5:11–13).

Yes, becoming a child of God, a Christian, is the essential first step to lasting joy. I trust that most of you reading this book have already taken that step. If you haven't, my prayer is that you will do so very soon—certainly before you finish reading this book. But please keep reading even if you have not yet made that decision because you have a right to know the satisfying, fulfilling life that can be yours.

As strange as it may seem, you can be a member of a church—you may even be a pastor or a church worker—and still not be a child of God. If you have never confessed your sin and accepted God's gift of new life, all the service to the church and all the good works in the world will not help you. I have known a number of pastors and missionaries, for instance, who realized *while in those positions* that they were not Christians. With the apostle Paul, I urge you to "examine yourselves as to whether you are in the faith" (2 Cor. 13:5).

The Big Picture

If it is true that God expects us to be servants—and it is—and if living the life of a servant is the key to lasting joy—which is also true—then we need to know just what's involved in being His servant. We've already seen that before anything else it means becoming His child through faith in Christ. But what else does it mean?

Being a servant of God means letting God work through you and living your life motivated by love for Him. A good summary of "the big picture" of the life of a servant is found in God's commissioning of the prophet Jeremiah. In chapter 1 of his book, Jeremiah tells how God ordained him to his ministry, and he mentions four aspects of his servanthood. Notice that in each case God initiates an action in Jeremiah's life, and that God's action is supposed to result in a life-changing difference in His servant's attitude and in the way he or she lives.

First, God told Jeremiah, "Before I formed you in the womb I knew you . . . and I ordained you a prophet to the nations" (v. 5). That's *a clear call to service.*

Second, God said to Jeremiah, "Before you were born I sancti-fied you" (v. 5). In that statement Jeremiah saw that God expected him to lead *a clean life.*

Third, in verse 9 God told the prophet, "Behold, I have put My words in your mouth." There's God's servant being given *a courageous message.*

Fourth, in verse 7 God said, "You shall go to all to whom I send you." God gives Jeremiah *a challenging purpose.*

The child of God who has committed to being the Lord's servant will hear a clear call, lead a clean life, proclaim a coura-geous message, and have a challenging purpose. This is the heart of what it means to be a servant of God. We will carefully examine each of these four aspects, seeing what they mean in the last years of the twentieth century, so that you will be better prepared to live in a way that God says will bring you lasting joy.

The Call to Servanthood

Now, you may think that the idea that *all* Christians are sup-posed to be servants is a bit strong. That's for missionaries, pas-tors, and other church leaders, isn't it? And besides, this book is supposed to be about how a life as God's servant is joy-filled, satisfying and fulfilling, isn't it? We're not supposed to get into such demanding stuff as what God *expects* of us, are we?

The fact is that giving our lives as servants of God is both what God expects *and* the only way to a life of lasting joy. Does that surprise you? It may, but it shouldn't. We have just considered how God, out of His great love for us, sent His Son to die in our place. We who are Christians are children of God because we have heard and responded to His call to us to be saved. Why, then, is it any surprise that the life to which He calls us is also the life that's the best for us? You may have accepted the idea that God hates fun and wants us always to be dour as we keep our noses pinned to the grindstone. But nothing could be further from the truth. Remember that both God's way of wisdom and the world's way of folly promise joy. Folly offers joy—joy for the moment. And folly is frequently more seductive and alluring. It has to be because it is empty and cannot provide true and long-lasting joy. It is only God's way of wisdom—by being His servant—that fulfills the promise and gives you lasting joy.

God clearly calls us in His Word to imitate the servant life of Jesus. Jesus told His disciples:

> You know that the rulers of the Gentiles lord it over them, and those who are great exercise authority over them. Yet it shall not be so among you; but whoever desires to become great among you, let him be your servant. And whoever desires to be first among you, let him be your slave—just as the Son of Man did not come to be served, but to serve, and to give His life a ransom for many (Matt. 20:25–28).

The apostle Paul put it this way:

> Let nothing be done through selfish ambition or conceit, but in lowliness of mind let each esteem others better than himself. Let each of you look out not only for his own interests, but also for the interests of others. Let this mind be in you which was also in Christ Jesus, who, being in the form of God, did not consider it robbery to be equal with God, but made Himself of no reputation, taking the form of a servant, and coming in the likeness of men (Phil. 2:3–7).

Jesus also said, "If anyone desires to come after Me, let him deny himself, and take up his cross daily, and follow me" (Luke 9:23). Paul's response was to say, "We do not preach ourselves, but Christ Jesus the Lord, and ourselves your servants for Jesus' sake" (2 Cor. 4:5).

These and many other scriptural passages I could quote make it very clear that in calling us to be His children, God has called us to be like His Son, the obedient servant. Jesus said, "I have come down from heaven, not to do My own will, but the will of Him who sent Me" (John 6:38). To be a Christian, a child of God, is to be a servant. It's that simple, and there is no way around it when you open your Bible and start reading.

The Basics

As we begin to examine what it means to be a servant, we need to understand that at the most basic level it's not a matter of what we do. Of course a servant serves, and that means action. But a true servant is a servant before he takes the first step to *do* anything.

A servant is ready to do whatever God asks because he recognizes he belongs to the Lord, not to himself, and so he is God's to command. The apostle Paul said, "Do you not know that your body is the temple of the Holy Spirit who is in you, whom you have from God, and you are not your own? For you were bought at a price; therefore glorify God in your body and in your spirit, which are God's" (1 Cor. 6:19–20).

On another occasion Paul said, "He [Jesus] died for all, that those who live should live no longer for themselves, but for Him who died for them and rose again" (2 Cor. 5:15).

The servant acknowledges that God bought him with Christ's blood, and thus he is always seeking God's will, always ready to do what the Lord asks. In contrast, the person who doesn't have a servant's heart seeks to have his own way. If he senses God wants him to do some particular thing, he will weigh the pros and cons and debate with himself before deciding one way or the other. But the servant always stands ready, *before* God asks, to do his Father's will. There is no question in his mind about what he should do when he is confident of God's direction.

Richard Foster speaks of this difference between the person who will serve out of self-centeredness and the person with a true servant's heart: "When we choose to serve we are still in charge. We decide whom we will serve and when we will serve. . . . But when we choose to be a servant we give up the right to be in charge. . . . We become available and vulnerable."[1]

Manford Gutzke, another insightful writer, put it this way: "It is not so much that a person hears the will of God . . . and then decides to do it. Rather, one yields himself to do the will of God, and then listens to see what it will be. It is an attitude that would look up to God and say, 'Speak, Lord, for thy servant heareth.'"[2]

This attitude of being yielded and available to God goes against our human tendency to want to run our own lives. And our modern culture that emphasizes "getting ahead" and "looking out for Number One" also opposes such submission. We should not be surprised that such opposition exists. That is folly speaking. But however difficult it may be to develop and maintain the attitude of a servant, we are not really servants at all unless we are striving to be submissive to our Lord.

Understand also that from God's perspective, our availability is far more important than our ability. If it is not your heart's desire to serve Him however and whenever He calls you, all the talent in the world is of no account in His eyes.

I am certain that God is far more pleased by Billy Graham's servant heart than He is by the number of miles Billy has traveled or the number of evangelistic sermons he has delivered. Now, if Billy's attitude were wrong, if he were motivated by pride or fought God's will every step of the way, the sovereign God could and probably would still work through Billy's life and words to some extent. But Billy himself would be displeasing to God. He would not be a servant. It's because Billy's heart is in the right place—not because of what he's done—that he is one of God's choicest servants.

Everyday Servants

Finally, let's consider one more facet of a servant's clear call. When we picture a "servant of God," we likely think of people like Billy Graham or a missionary over in Africa whom we once met. Perhaps your mind turns to some of the great saints of the early church who gave their lives courageously as martyrs for the faith.

The common element in all these pictures is that we tend to think of people who do extraordinary things or who have made the ultimate sacrifice of their lives. At the least, we tend to see a servant as someone out of the normal stream of life and work, someone who devotes full time to "Christian work"—someone like your pastor.

However, God calls *all* His people to be servants because He wants all of us to have lasting joy. And surely all of us aren't called to become evangelists, missionaries, or martyrs. God needs His servants to be in every town and in every line of endeavor—engineers, truck drivers, salespeople, cooks, factory workers, and accountants. He wants us to serve Him right where we are in our families, our churches, our neighborhoods, our schools, our places of work.

Moreover, the test of our servanthood is not in some dramatic, once-in-a-lifetime event like being forced to deny Christ or face execution (although our brothers and sisters in Christ in other parts of the world often do have to make such a choice). Rather, we're called to think and act like servants in the routine, mundane events of our daily lives.

When we're tired and our children are driving us up the wall, will we still serve them with God's love? When the boss is making our day miserable, will we still "obey in all things your masters . . . not with eye service, as men-pleasers, but in sincerity of heart, fearing God" (Col. 3:22)? These areas are where the courage of a servant is tested.

This need to be servants in the routine of life is not glamorous, which is one reason we would prefer to avoid it. As Richard Foster says, "In some ways we would prefer to hear Jesus' call to deny father and mother, houses and land for the sake of the gospel, than His word to wash feet. Radical self-denial gives the feel of adventure. If we forsake all, we even have the chance of glorious martyrdom. But in service we are banished to the mundane, the ordinary, the trivial."[3] But it is in serving that we experience joy, and being servants in the routine of life lets us know the joy of the Lord daily.

Another reason we wish servanthood were more glamorous is that such an approach appeals to our natural laziness. If servanthood is reserved for rare, extraordinary events, or is only for "supersaints," we are free to take it easy the rest of the time—which, practically speaking, is *most* of the time. As author and pastor Charles Swindoll put it, "This decision to give ourselves to others (taking up our cross) has to be a *daily* matter. That's costly stuff. Terribly expensive."[4]

Finally, we tend not to think of servanthood as involving the routine affairs of life because we have underestimated their importance. Manford Gutzke correctly said, "The servant of God may be a very ordinary looking person and with a very ordinary manner of life."[5] But will that person's life or death receive as much publicity as that of the Christian celebrity? No, of course not. A life of faithful, loving service that quietly touches everyone around it just isn't valued as highly as the life of a famous person.

When we look at life from God's perspective, however, we see that the small choices we make every day are the ones that shape our lives and those of the people around us. We begin to understand that consistent availability to the Lord is far more valuable than the occasional flash of the talented but self-serving person. Richard Foster summarized this so well: "In the realm of the spirit we soon discover that the real issues are found in the tiny insignificant corners of life. Our infatuation with the 'big deal' has blinded us to this fact. . . . [But] we will come to see small things as the *central* issues" (italics mine).[6]

As you consider the life of a servant, are you willing to be God's person right where you are now, in the tasks and relationships that are already the substance of your life? That's not glamorous—there may be no monuments erected in your honor. But that's what it means to be a servant.

Like Jeremiah, each of God's servants receives a clear call. God told Jeremiah, "Before I formed you in the womb I knew you . . . and I ordained you a prophet to the nations." If you are to be a servant of God, you will receive His clear call, too. First, and above all else, you will be called to become a child of God through faith in Jesus Christ. Then too, as a Christian you will be called to be a servant. God makes no exceptions; it's what He expects, and it's the key to the most fulfilling and joy-filled life we can experience. It is therefore vital to know what it means to be a servant.

We've seen that servanthood is more a matter of attitude than action, that God wants our availability more than our talent, and that for most of us servanthood means faithfulness in the ordinary affairs of everyday living.

Having said all that, we must realize, too, that servanthood will be demonstrated in the way a person lives, different ways for different people. Many Christians believe that all servants of God are called to the same kind of life and work. That's not true, however—a lesson my son helped me learn.

1. Richard Foster, *Celebration of Discipline* (New York, San Francisco: Harper & Row, 1978), p. 115.
2. Manford George Gutzke, *Born to Serve* (Glendale, CA: Regal, 1972), p. 51.
3. Foster, p. 110.
4. Charles R. Swindoll, *Improving Your Serve* (Waco, TX: Word Books, 1981), p. 48.
5. Gutzke, p. 22.
6. Foster, p. 118.

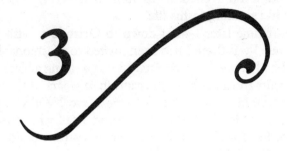

3

NO COOKIE CUTTERS, PLEASE

WHEN MY SON JIM was the assistant pastor at the large First Baptist Church in Orlando, Florida, he felt called to start a ministry among the drug addicts and hippies there. He and some folks working with him set up a building in a part of the city frequented by those kinds of people, and they began to invite them in off the streets to hear the gospel. The name they gave this place was The Good Thief.

As Jim's father, I wasn't too thrilled when I heard he was starting this ministry, even though he was full of enthusiasm as he would tell me about it. It didn't fit my idea of how one went about evangelizing.

Besides that, I didn't want my son to become known as a "hippie preacher." I was afraid he would get identified that way, and then he would never be taken seriously in any other kind of ministry. So one night I said to him on the phone, "Son, let me tell you something as your daddy. You've got a bigger ministry than that." And I encouraged him to look for other ways to follow God's calling in his life.

A short time later I went down to Orlando to visit Jim. One night while I was there I had been invited to a fashionable dinner, and so I had dressed appropriately. I was wearing a black suit with a white shirt and a black tie. Jim came in to see me at the end of the dinner and said, "Dad, will you do me a favor? Will you just come down to The Good Thief and see for yourself what goes on?"

I agreed and went with him to the downtown building, which was just about a block from his church. When I first saw it from the outside, all my worst fears about the place were confirmed. There was psychedelic paint everywhere, and the lighting was dim, to put it mildly.

Going inside didn't do anything to make me feel any better. There were people lying all over the floor, and I didn't know if they had been smoking pot or what. The walls inside were covered with crazy-looking paint, too, although the message it spelled out were things like "Jesus Loves You" and "Christ Died for Our Sins." The man in front who was speaking to the crowd called the place where he was standing "the God ramp."

I was trying to take all this in and gain my composure when the speaker announced that the Reverend T. W. Wilson had just walked in. Would I come down onto the God ramp and talk to them for a while, he asked?

Frankly, I would have preferred not to do it. Here I was dressed up and as out of place as it was possible to be. On top of that, I knew that being introduced as "the Reverend" didn't exactly endear me to that audience. But I also felt I didn't have any choice. After all, he had already introduced me. And besides, I *am* an evangelist. So I tried to get my thoughts together, and I fervently asked the Lord to help me even more than usual.

That night several very difficult lives were transformed by the Spirit of God. I knew these were people who weren't likely to drop in on a church, and the Lord had used me to help reach them.

What could I say to Jim after that? He had been right about his ministry, and I had been totally wrong in judging it before I even saw it. I told him, "Jim, your daddy has been very, very stupid. You keep on doing what God called you to do."

I tell this story to illustrate one simple point. God has given each of His servants a clear call: a clear call to salvation and a clear call to service. For each of us, that call is unique and personal. God deals with each of us in a way that is particularly suited to our personality and to God's purpose for us—in a way that is different from the way He calls others of His servants.

Your call to salvation may be different from mine. God probably used different circumstances to save you. Too frequently, however, we expect God to work the same way all the time. I like to imagine two men talking—both had been blind and both had been given their sight by Jesus Christ. One tells how Jesus spat on the ground, made mud of the spittle, put it on his eyes, and told him to wash it off. "There's no sight without mud," he might insist. The second man relates how Jesus simply touched him, restored his sight, and told him to sin no more. "You're wrong. Jesus gave me my sight without mud." The two might even start two denominations! The fact is, however, that God works in different ways with different people.

Just as God's call to salvation is unique and personal, so is His call to service. God does not cut out His servants with a cookie cutter. We are not all supposed to be the same and He does not want us all to serve others in the same way.

A Natural Tendency

All of us, however, want people to be like us. It's a natural tendency. We're uncomfortable around others who are noticeably different from us, and we tend to think secretly that the world would be a whole lot better off if everyone were just a little more like us.

Think of the last party you attended. There was probably at least one person there who really bothered you. Perhaps this person was very loud, and you're reserved. Maybe he wore a bright paisley tie with a bold plaid sportcoat, and you had to fight the urge to give him a quick lesson in tasteful dressing. Or maybe she was ignorant of some of the social graces, and you were embarrassed for her.

Regardless of how unfair and unloving it is for us to evaluate people by these kinds of criteria, we tend to do it all the time. And when others are found wanting in our judgments, their failures are usually in areas where we perceive them to be different from ourselves.

On the other hand, people who meet with our approval are generally those we perceive to be like us (or like what we dream of being). They share our tastes in music, keep up their homes as well as we do, think like us in political affairs, and drive down the road as confidently or cautiously as we drive.

Now when it comes to matters of religious faith, this natural human tendency is multiplied. Added to the usual feelings is a righteous conviction that our ways of thinking and living are more in line with God's plan than anyone else's.

Please don't misunderstand what I'm saying at this point. Of course there's only one way to a right relationship with God, and that's through Jesus Christ (as outlined in chapter 2). The problem arises, however, when we insist that God's call to salvation and service has to be the same for everyone. My experience with Jim is a perfect example of this. I had one idea of what it meant to be a pastor and to evangelize people. Jim, growing up in a different era and with different experiences, had another idea that he thought would work better with the kind of people he wanted to reach.

But because Jim's idea was different from mine, because he didn't fit my mold, I assumed he was wrong without even checking out what he was accomplishing. To my mind, he needed to be doing his ministry the way I thought best. I had my Christian cookie cutter in hand, and he didn't fit.

The Biblical Perspective

The apostle Paul encountered some people in his day who thought every Christian was called to the same ministry. He pointed out the problem with that viewpoint by comparing the church, all believers in Christ everywhere, with a body that needs many different parts. He put it this way:

> For as the body is one and has many members, but all the members of that one body, being many, are one body, so also is Christ. For by one Spirit we were all baptized into one body—whether Jews or Greeks, whether slaves or free—and have all been made to drink into one Spirit. For in fact the body is not one member but many. If the foot should say, "Because I am not a hand, I am not of the body," is it therefore not of the body? And if the ear should say, "Because I am not an eye, I am not of the body," is it therefore not of the body? If the whole body were an eye, where would be the hearing? If the whole were hearing, where would be the smelling? But now God has set the members, each one of them, in the body just as He pleased. And if they were all one member, where would the body be? But now indeed there are many members, yet one body. And the eye cannot say to the hand, "I have no need of you"; nor again the head to the feet, "I have no need of you."

What Paul was saying is simply that in order for the church to function properly, it needs all kinds of people doing different kinds of work. It needs people like Billy Graham evangelizing on a mass scale. It needs local pastors and Bible teachers building up believers. It needs people like my son Jim reaching out to specific kinds of people. It needs Franklin Graham of Samaritan's Purse (and many others like him), who offers food to hungry people around the world in the name and with the love of Jesus.

The cause of Christ also requires doctors, teachers, brick masons, secretaries, and other lay people who are serving God in the secular world, being salt and light to those around them.

To borrow a business term, the bottom line is this: you should not expect everyone, including other believers, to be like you in every way, nor should they demand that you be like them. Each servant of God has received a clear call, but that call is different for each of us. Heaven help us if the world were full of T. W. Wilsons—or of carbon copies of you!

Manford Gutzke expressed this idea as follows: "Christians differ from each other. They are as different as we have many members in one body. . . . All members have not the same office. Everyone does not do the same thing. . . . Each member will do as the Lord wishes him to do, and together they will perform the will of God."[1]

This toleration of differences among believers should also include differences in nonessential areas of doctrine. God's calling in my life led me to be a Baptist; God may have called you to be a Lutheran. That will mean that we differ on certain doctrines. All biblical doctrine is important, of course, but let's recognize that some truths are central to our faith and not open to debate, whereas others are secondary and open for discussion. What matters most is that we agree on the person and work of Jesus Christ. If we have that common ground, I will call you my brother or sister regardless of, for example, how you baptize or whether you use wine or grape juice in the Communion service.

Issues like the mode of baptism do matter, of course, and we all choose to join churches whose views on such questions we can support. You no doubt are convinced that the beliefs of your church are most consistent with biblical teaching. Does it surprise you that I feel the same way about my beliefs? The point is that differences of opinion on these secondary issues are bound to exist, and neither of us should insist that the other change before fellowship is possible. The bond we have in Christ should be stronger than the division between us over secondary issues because we recognize that God's calling to each Christian is unique and personal.

The Importance of Spiritual Gifts

One way we can see the difference in the calls to service of God's servants is in the different gifts that He has given by His

Spirit for the proper functioning of the church. Different people have different gifts. The apostle Paul said, "There are diversities of gifts, but the same Spirit. There are differences of ministries, but the same Lord. And there are diversities of activities, but it is the same God who works all in all. But the manifestation of the Spirit is given to each one for the profit of all. . . . But one and the same Spirit works all these things, distributing to each one individually as He wills" (1 Cor. 12:4–7, 11).

It is immediately after this passage that Paul made the comparison between the church and a body that was quoted earlier. There is a need for diversity in the work of the church. Thus, because of the different spiritual gifts we have—notice that Paul said the Spirit distributes gifts "to each one individually"—we will have different perspectives and priorities in our Christian lives. And that's good.

For example, a person who has the gift of teaching will likely want to see the church stress the importance of strong Bible teaching. On the other hand, a person with the gift of mercy may well want the church to major in a ministry that meets the physical and emotional needs of people in the name of Christ. Neither of these people is wrong in his emphasis; both contribute in their own ways to the life of the church and help it to keep a well-rounded perspective.

There are several places in the Bible where spiritual gifts are listed (see 1 Cor. 12:8–10 and Rom. 12:6–8), and biblical scholars have found other gifts in other passages. Just how many gifts there are is not definite—the number you come up with depends on whose book you read or whose sermon you listen to. One gift which scholars have identified is the gift of martyrdom, and I think it's safe to say that's the gift for which there are the fewest volunteers!

My purpose here is not to discuss the gifts themselves or help you identify which you have. Other fine books can assist you in doing that. What I do want to stress, however, is that God's unique call to service includes giving you certain gifts. As a servant it's important for you to discern what spiritual gifts you have and develop and use them in His service. To ignore your spiritual gifts and not use them will lead to frustration. To identify them and use them fully will lead to joy. The spiritual gifts God has given you are an important part of your calling and a key part of what will make your ministry different from that of many other Christians.

No Lookalikes, Either

The story I told at the beginning of this chapter about what I learned from Jim and the Lord isn't the only lesson I gained from that trip to Florida. The day after my visit to The Good Thief, Jim wanted to take his dad fishing, and God knew I needed another session on allowing people to be different from me.

So Jim, the chairman of his board, and I went out to one of the lakes near Orlando. I bought a temporary fishing license, we got some worms for bait, and we were going to rent a small boat from which to do our fishing.

As you can imagine, Jim was not in the habit of dressing like me. And one of the things he was wearing then was a big, *big* fish symbol on a chain around his neck. Naturally, I did not approve; I considered it to be in poor taste for a pastor. In fact, as with my earlier concern about the nature of his ministry, I was looking for the right time to give him a bit of fatherly wisdom on the matter.

Well, there were several other men in the bait and tackle store that morning, and after a few minutes one of them asked Jim, "Hey, pal, what's that you've got around your neck?"

Jim answered, "Sir, this is a fish. You know, back in the early days of the Christian church they used the fish as one of their identifying symbols, along with the cross. Today most Christians use a cross, but I just prefer to use the fish."

The man looked interested, and so Jimmy went on. "Sir, do you know why I wear this fish? I do it so that I can tell everyone who asks about it, just as you have, what the Lord Jesus Christ means to me." And then he explained how the letters in the Greek word for "fish" form an acronym for a series of names of Jesus: Jesus Christ, God's Son, Our Savior. Finally he said, "By the way, mister, are you a Christian?"

The man responded, "No, but I guess I ought to be."

Meanwhile, down at the other end of the counter in this store, the chairman of Jim's board, a layman in the insurance business, struck up a conversation with another man who had overheard what Jim was saying. This man said to the chairman, "You know, I like that." And with that opening, the chairman began to talk to him about Christ.

Well, I saw what was happening and thought I ought to be doing something too! So I asked a third man what he thought about what Jimmy was saying, and he said, "You know, I like that young fellow. I wish I knew what made him tick."

I answered, "As his father, maybe I can tell you a little about that."

The simple conclusion to this story is that when Jim, the chairman of his board, and I walked out of the store that morning full of joy, there were three men inside who had accepted Christ and whom I look forward to seeing in heaven—all because my young son dared to wear a fish around his neck. I told him after we left, "Jim, you go on wearing that fish—wear a bigger one if you want to!"

There are several lessons we can learn from that experience, one of them being that when God wants to teach me something, He probably needs to give me the message more than once before it really sinks in. But the more important lesson is that not only do God's servants have different types of ministries, but they will also look different, and that's OK. I hadn't liked that fish symbol Jim wore. I thought it was improper, and so I wanted him to get rid of it. But God saw it very differently, and it was a part of Jim's unique and very effective ministry.

So much of what we think is part of being a "proper" Christian is really cultural Christianity, which is another way of saying it is legalism. And that's another way of saying that because we think we've got the Christian life all figured out, we like to go into every area of one another's lives and prescribe how they should think, act, and talk. Is that biblical? Could I have quoted Jim chapter and verse on why he shouldn't wear a fish symbol on a chain around his neck? Of course not. Such legalism is not biblical, and it's not right.

You may not like the cut of my clothes. I may not like the length of your hair or your skirt. You may drive a car that another believer would consider too sporty or too luxurious for a "dedicated Christian." But none of those things is as important as a person's relationship with God through Jesus Christ. Let Him work in your life and conscience and give you a ministry uniquely suited to you. But you should also give Him the freedom to work uniquely in the rest of us, too.

The late Arthur DeMoss was a very wealthy man. He founded his own insurance company and built it into a huge success. Even though he gave away millions of dollars to various Christian organizations, he was still able to live very well in suburban Philadelphia. Because he was so successful in his work, he had regular contact with many other highly successful business people—the so-called "up and outers" who are seldom reached by most Christian ministries.

To reach these people for Christ, Art and his wife, Nancy, started a ministry that was unique at the time. They would invite some of their wealthy acquaintances to dinner at their beautiful home, and after the meal they would bring in a speaker who was also very successful in his field—someone like Coach Tom Landry of the Dallas Cowboys football team. The speaker would then give a simple, clear presentation of the gospel and of what Christ meant in his or her life.

Through this ministry, and through the many contacts Art had with people as he traveled on business, literally thousands of people came to a saving faith in Jesus Christ. And the ministry continues today through the Arthur S. DeMoss Foundation, which Art started and endowed before he passed away.

What's my point in telling you about Art and Nancy DeMoss? To some people like Art and Nancy, God entrusts great wealth. And they, being faithful and fruitful servants, use that money to minister in a unique and most effective way. God may not give you that kind of financial prosperity, but your ministry and your lifestyle, whatever they are, can be uniquely used by God in equally fruitful service if you're willing to give your life to Him.

What matters is not how we look or talk or where we live, but where our hearts are.

The Freedom of Uniqueness

Finally, let me point out something I hope you've already begun to realize as you've read this chapter. The central truth I've been trying to get across—that we're not all supposed to be alike, that God calls each of us uniquely—is a tremendously freeing thing. If we will concentrate on what God wants us to be and do, we will be free to be and do those things.

That means we'll be free from the expectations of others!

Learn what spiritual gifts you've been given. Study yourself to see how God has made you. Take time with Him, and also talk to wise Christians who know you well, so you can discern those few areas to which God is specifically calling you in service at this point in your life. Then go after those things with all your might and with all your love, and give your brothers and sisters in Christ the opportunity to do the same. If you do, you'll soon know a freedom and joy that before was only a part of your dreams.

---

1. Manford George Gutzke, *Born to Serve* (Glendale, CA: Regal, 1972), pp. 86–87.

4

CALLED

IN STRENGTH

WHEN I FIRST BEGAN my ministry as an evangelist many years ago, before I joined Billy Graham's team, I was given the opportunity to preach in a large crusade organized by one hundred cooperating churches in Grand Rapids, Michigan. They already had singers and everybody else they needed lined up, and they wanted me to be the speaker.

Now, what I had heard about Grand Rapids didn't make me eager to go there. I knew that Calvinism in this country had been born in that city, and it was (and still is) strongly Calvinistic territory. I knew, too, that the average lay person there takes his theology very seriously. And I knew that in Grand Rapids if you want to tell a joke from the pulpit—something I enjoy doing—you've almost got to have a Bible in your hand.

All these thoughts went through my mind when I received the phone call about the crusade to be held there. At that time, I was already very sure of God's clear call on my life and service. Both my wife and I knew that I was to be an evangelist. However, as I considered my inadequacies in light of the well-educated, expert theological audience I expected to face in Grand Rapids, I decided that that was not the place for a young evangelist like me. Without telling the people there why, I declined their invitation.

My wife, who is my best friend and my sweetheart, is also my best critic, and she doesn't mince any words with me. When I hung up the phone after turning down the people in Grand Rapids, she asked, "Why did you tell them you couldn't come?"

"You just don't understand Grand Rapids," I said, and I explained some of what I had been thinking.

She said, "Darling, I must say with all my love for you that I am disappointed and shocked. Are you depending upon the Holy Spirit of God to make that crusade successful, or are you depending upon your own strength?"

I didn't want to admit it, but she had really hit me in the heart with those words. So I said, "You just don't understand."

Well, God was in this thing, and so I wasn't going to get off that easily. The people from Grand Rapids called me back, and they said, "We have some options on the dates for the crusade. When can you come?"

Because I still didn't relish the prospect of speaking to such a sophisticated, well-informed audience, I replied, "I have to tell you that I really don't think I'm the man you're looking for."

They said, "Let us take a chance on that. When can you come?"

I finally reached the point of feeling I had no choice but to go, so I went to Grand Rapids with much fear and trembling. And in spite of this weak, fearful, reluctant servant, God did a wonderful work in the city through that crusade. The results were the exact opposite of what I had expected, and the whole crusade was an experience I'll never forget.

A Servant's Strength Comes from the Master

This story about the early days of my ministry illustrates the central point of this chapter. I was wrong to resist going to Grand Rapids, and my error was in counting only on my own strength and abilities. I counted *my* resources of education and eloquence and felt they were inadequate, but I didn't even consider that God was in that crusade and that if He were calling me, He would give me the strength I needed to be an effective servant. My beloved wife had hit the nail right on the head.

The point is that when God gives you a clear call He is also ready to give you His strength to see it through, and that if you try to do what He calls you to do on your own, you are bound to fail. We must serve in *His* strength or we are heading for frustration. Jesus put this so well and so simply when He said, "Abide in Me, and I in you. As the branch cannot bear fruit of itself, unless it abides in the vine, neither can you, unless you abide in Me. I am the vine, you are the branches. He who abides in Me, and I in him, bears much fruit; for without Me you can do nothing" (John 15:4–5).

Let me show you both by biblical teaching and by examples how God gives to those He calls the strength to do tasks that may otherwise seem impossible. Let me also show you how He expects us to depend on His strength, not our own.

Being called by God means that we have the reassuring promise that God's strength is always available to us. One of the psalmists wrote, "God is our refuge and strength, a very present help in trouble. Therefore we will not fear, though the earth be removed, and though the mountains be carried into the midst of the sea" (Ps. 46:1–2).

The prophet Isaiah wrote, "Those who wait on the Lord shall renew their strength; they shall mount up with wings like eagles, they shall run and not be weary, they shall walk and not faint" (40:31). A few verses later he spoke for God and said, "Fear not, for I am with you; be not dismayed, for I am your God. I will strengthen you, yes, I will help you, I will uphold you with My righteous right hand" (41:10).

Jesus promised His disciples that the Holy Spirit would be with them to give them power after He left this earth: "You shall receive power when the Holy Spirit has come upon you" (Acts 1:8). And Paul the apostle frequently prayed that the churches to which he ministered would be filled with this strength, or power, as when he prayed for the Colossians that they would be "strengthened with all might, according to His glorious power" (Col. 1:11).

The experience of Jesus' own disciples is one of the best examples of the difference God's strength through the Holy Spirit makes in believers' lives. Before His death, you will remember, the disciples argued among themselves about who was the greatest and who would have the place of highest honor in His kingdom—in other words, they were hardly spiritual giants. And when their fantasies were shattered on the night He was betrayed and arrested, they all ran away in terror and hid, afraid the authorities would come after them, too.

On the Day of Pentecost, however, they were filled with supernatural power, and neither they nor the world were ever the same again. They began by turning Jerusalem upside down with their powerful preaching and the testimony of their Christian love. When Peter and John were taken before the Sanhedrin, the same religious leaders who condemned Jesus ordered them to stop preaching in the name of Jesus. What was their response? Did they run and hide again? Indeed they did not! They prayed, "Now, Lord, look on their threats, and grant to Your servants that with all boldness they may speak Your word. . . . And when they had prayed, the place where they were assembled together was shaken . . . and they spoke the word of God with boldness" (Acts 4:29, 31). The strength of God applied to their lives made a phenomenal difference.

Paul spoke often of the effects of God's strength in his own life. In Philippians 4:13 he said, "I can do all things through Christ who strengthens me." In his first letter to the Thessalonians he wrote, "For our gospel did not come to you in word only, but also in power, and in the Holy Spirit and in much assurance, as you know what kind of men we were among you for your sake" (1:5).

And to his own disciple Timothy he said, "For God has not given us a spirit of fear, but of power and of love and of a sound mind" (2 Tim. 1:7).

Paul also spoke in his letter to the Roman Christians about the futility of his efforts to defeat sin in his life with his own strength. And what was the source of victory? "I thank God—through Jesus Christ our Lord!" (7:25). Over and over again, God promises strength to those whom He calls.

When I think of God's strength being given and displayed in times of adversity, my mind turns to Gerry and Nancy Gardner. Nancy is the daughter of my brother Grady, and she and her husband, Gerry, were serving as missionaries in Colombia, where Gerry was a pilot with Wycliffe Bible Translators.

The first tragedy they suffered was when their small son died from croup down in Colombia. It was a hard thing for them to take, as you might imagine. But then on top of that, Chet Bitterman, another missionary in Bogotá and a good friend of Gerry's, was murdered. Gerry had to fly Chet's body to the South American city of Loma Linda, Colombia, and they buried him right next to Gerry and Nancy's son.

As Gerry stood in the cemetery watching the workmen lower Chet's coffin into the grave, he looked up and cried out in prayer, "Oh God, how much more is it going to cost to get Your Word to these people?"

In that moment, Gerry sensed God saying to his spirit, "Gerry, it has already cost Me My only begotten Son."

Those words filled Gerry's heart with a fresh sense of peace and strength, and he replied, "All right, Lord, whatever you say. I know that your purposes are always right, even when we don't understand." Gerry left that place a stronger man, a more mature and determined servant of His Savior.

To God Must Be the Glory

Being called by God also means that we seek to glorify Him by living in His strength. When we serve God in our own strength, we will subtly think we can take the credit. But when we serve

Him in His strength, He'll receive the glory for what He does in and through us.

It's not easy for us to step aside and rely on God's strength, and then give Him the glory for what is accomplished. Our pride gets in the way. And because of that, we usually go through a process of learning—of trial and error—before we're willing to lean on Him. Many times this means trying on our own and failing. But whether we go through that painful process or not, we must somehow come to the realization that not only can we not serve God in our own strength, but our first task as servants is to glorify the Master.

Before the apostle Paul became a Christian, he was a devout, well-educated, and self-righteous man. He said of himself in Philippians 3, "If anyone else thinks he may have confidence in the flesh, I more so: circumcised the eighth day, of the stock of Israel, of the tribe of Benjamin, a Hebrew of the Hebrews; concerning the law, a Pharisee; concerning zeal, persecuting the church; concerning the righteousness which is in the law, blameless" (vv. 4–6). Paul was a man who had reason to be self-confident!

But what was Paul's attitude toward those things that gave him his confidence? "What things were gain to me, these I have counted loss for Christ" (Phil. 3:7). And how did he come to feel that way? Through a lot of painful learning. In Galatians 1, Paul wrote that after his conversion, he did not immediately begin missionary work. Instead, the Lord gave him a three-year course in theology and the Christian life (see vv. 14–18). During that time he began to learn lessons that he continued to learn and relearn, I'm sure, throughout his life.

One of Paul's hard-learned lessons dealt with living in adversity. In 2 Corinthians 12 he talked about his "thorn in the flesh" and how he pleaded with God to remove it three times. But God wouldn't remove it and instead said to Paul, "My grace is sufficient for you, for My strength is made perfect in weakness" (v. 9). In other words, God told Paul, "I'm going to leave you weak in this area, though I'll give you grace to bear it. But because you have this weakness, you'll have to lean on Me and My strength. And because you will, you and the rest of the world will constantly see that your strength and your effectiveness are from Me, not from yourself."

What was Paul's response? His marvelous answer did not come easily, I'm sure. It has the wisdom of a lesson learned the hard way: "Therefore most gladly I will rather boast in my infirmities, that the power of Christ may rest upon me. Therefore I take pleasure in infirmities, in reproaches, in needs, in persecutions, in distresses, for Christ's sake. For when I am weak, then I am strong [in Him]" (2 Cor. 12:9-10). Paul knew he was called by God and wanted to glorify Him by living in His strength.

This is difficult stuff, isn't it? Would you gladly accept weakness, reproach, persecution, and distress in order to let God's strength be demonstrated in your life? Would I? Yet that's exactly the attitude Paul had and toward which we should be striving. The crucial point here is that in all we are and do God must be glorified. His servants who hear His clear call will gladly live in God's strength—not their own—so that God may be glorified. They will do this even when it is costly and difficult. But believe me when I say that in doing this you will find lasting joy—and that's worth all the cost and all the difficulty.

The importance of God's being glorified is nowhere more important than in the spread of the gospel, and Paul told us that this even influences whom God calls to be His children and servants.

To those who are called, both Jews and Greeks, Christ [is] the power of God and the wisdom of God. Because the foolishness of God is wiser than men, and the weakness of God is stronger than men. For you see your calling, brethren, that not many wise according to the flesh, not many mighty, not many noble, are called. But God has chosen the foolish things of the world to put to shame the wise, and God has chosen the weak things of the world to put to shame the things which are mighty; and the base things of the world and the things which are despised God has chosen, and the things which are not, to bring to nothing the things that are, *that no flesh should glory in His presence* (1 Cor. 1:24-29, italics mine).

It is vital that God receive the glory due His name. When the world sees a servant who has a clear call and whose strength in carrying out that call comes from the Lord, glory is given where it belongs.

Strength from Who We Are

It is true that the servant of God is to glorify God, not himself, and it is also true that a cardinal virtue of the child of God is humility—an idea we'll discuss in the next chapter. But we must balance those truths by realizing that being called by God means realizing our worth as His children. Realizing our worth will let us put God's strength into practice.

There is a strain of teaching in the Christian world that emphasizes that we're all awful sinners. No matter how much we love the Lord, no matter how faithfully and sincerely we try to follow Him and please Him, we are told to focus our attention on how bad and sinful we are. Don't get me wrong. In chapter 2, we saw that we are all sinners who come short of the glory of God, and that salvation comes only by His grace.

The problem comes when we focus on our sinfulness to the practical exclusion of appreciation for God's grace and what we have become by it. We also saw in chapter 2 that when we receive Christ into our lives we become children of the heavenly Father, princes and princesses in the family of the great King. Paul said this so clearly in his letter to the Galatians: "For you are all sons of God through faith in Christ Jesus. . . . God sent forth His Son . . . that we might receive the adoption as sons. And because you are sons, God has sent forth the Spirit of His Son into your hearts, crying out, 'Abba, Father!' Therefore you are no longer a slave but a son, and if a son, then an heir of God through Christ" (3:26; 4:4–7).

Because we have been adopted into God's family, we should draw on His strength and follow His calling with confidence. We should live like the children of a sovereign King.

What happens when Christians always focus on their sinfulness, however, is that they become easily convinced they're worthless and incapable of accomplishing anything for the kingdom of God.

And because what we think about ourselves leads directly to the way we live, these Christians *make themselves* ineffective as servants of the Lord.

It should come as no surprise that Satan encourages Christians to focus constantly on their sinfulness rather than on the fact of God's forgiveness. Author Dave Seamands identifies clearly this tactic of the enemy:

> Satan's greatest psychological weapon is a gut-feeling of inferiority, inadequacy, and low self-worth. This feeling shackles many Christians, in spite of wonderful spiritual experiences, in spite of their faith and knowledge of God's Word. . . . They are tied up in knots, bound by a terrible feeling of inferiority, and chained to a deep sense of worthlessness.[1]

Chuck Swindoll echoed this truth when he wrote, "It is doubtful that anyone who wrestles with an unhealthy self-image can correctly and adequately give to others."[2]

The people to whom Seamands referred have heard and know *intellectually* that by faith in Christ they are forgiven and are children of God. But because they dwell on their sinfulness and worthlessness, the truth of their adoption into God's family has not reached their *hearts* and so has failed to affect their daily lives. The result is a lot of unhappy believers who are also weak and ineffective servants.

Brothers and sisters in Christ, we are children of the living God. We are joint heirs with Christ! That ought to be a tremendous encouragement to you, as it is to me. He has called us into His family and given us a part in His work on this earth. Let's claim His strength for the task and get on with it.

Strength to Face Opposition

Why do I stress the need for God's strength in following His call? I do so because if you don't live in God's strength, you are liable to end up a confused, hurt, discouraged servant. Being called by God means, first of all, that we have the reassuring promise that God's strength is always available to us. It also means that we are to live in His strength because doing so will glorify our Master. Third, since we are called by God, we are to realize our worth, and that realization will let us put God's strength into practice. His strength is necessary for two reasons: to face opposition and to survive prosperity.

Simply put, the more you try to serve God, the more opposition you can expect to encounter. Some of it will come from sources you'd expect, but some of it will take you by surprise if you don't realize the way the world works. I want us to look at three sources of opposition for which we will need God's strength.

The most obvious cause of opposition to God's servants is Satan. Satan seeks to thwart the work and the people of God wherever, whenever, and however he can. He is the embodiment of dark evil, and he stands in total opposition to God's holy light. Jesus described Satan this way: "He was a murderer from the beginning, and does not stand in the truth, because there is no truth in him. When he speaks a lie, he speaks from his own resources, for he is a liar and the father of it" (John 8:44).

The apostle Peter warned, "Be sober, be vigilant; because your adversary the devil walks about like a roaring lion, seeking whom he may devour" (1 Peter 5:8).

What form can you expect satanic opposition to take? First, Satan may oppose you through people who are his servants (whether they realize it or not). Also, as much as we might prefer to avoid this truth, the fact is that there are many ungodly people in the world who oppose God and violate His principles. They are serving Satan even if they don't think of themselves in that way. Pornographers, drug dealers, and child molesters are only some of the more obvious people to whom I refer.

Although in seeking to serve Christ you may encounter some of the types of people I just mentioned, it is far more likely that you will face opposition from people who are less menacing but who are serving the cause of Satan nonetheless. For example, suppose you have been witnessing to a co-worker in your office or plant. Don't be surprised if another co-worker, perhaps an atheist or a member of a cult, overhears your conversation and tries to disrupt it or to talk your co-worker out of becoming a Christian. That person is serving Satan's purpose.

Second, Satan may oppose you by bringing temptation into your life to draw you away from God, destroy your faith, and ruin your effectiveness as a servant. Here again, while you may encounter an obvious temptation toward gross sinfulness—such as an invitation to adultery from a member of the opposite sex— Satan is usually much more subtle and cunning in his attacks on believers. Jesus described him as a master liar, and he is constantly seeking to convince Christians to believe something less than God's truth.

How does Satan go about this? He will begin by seeking to create just a little doubt or cause you to question just how serious a sin really is for which he knows you have a weakness. As Manford Gutzke wrote, "The devil does not openly contradict God, but he suggests to the mind of the person being tempted that God's commandment need not be taken too seriously. . . . The form of any temptation will depend on the personal character and training of the individual being tempted."[3]

Satan will also try to get you to doubt the Bible, because it is the Christian servant's guidebook and the depository of God's truth. As Gutzke again said, "If he [Satan] can get the believer to doubt the Word of God, he is separating the believer from the Word of God, and therefore from his Lord. That leaves the believer on his own, alone. When the believer is alone, he is no match for the devil."[4]

Because Satan also knows that God's servants are a threat to him only when they act in God's strength, he will further tempt you to seek to serve God on your own, apart from God's will and strength. In this way you will think you are obediently serving God while you are in fact working from your own weakness, perhaps still doing God's business, but certainly not in His way. You will become ineffective in your service, and Satan will have accomplished his purpose.

I have wanted to acquaint you with some of Satan's tactics so they won't catch you unaware and so you will realize the importance of staying close to the Lord and drawing on His strength for your service. While we are no match for Satan, *he* is no match for our God, and according to the book of Revelation, Satan's eventual destruction is assured.

A second source of opposition that we need God's strength to overcome is our own sinful nature, which the Bible commonly calls "the flesh." I'm sure you are aware of the struggle that goes on within each of us daily between the spiritual nature we received as part of our adoption into God's family and the old, rebellious nature we inherited from our forefather Adam. This sinful nature is lazy, selfish, and generally opposed to the will of God, and so we need to call upon God's strength for victory.

Be careful not to underestimate the corrupting power of the human sinful nature. As writer Larry Maddox has observed, it can easily lead people to join churches for the worst possible reason: "People always seem to be doing something either *for* self, *with* self, or *to* self. Even religion has become a selfish influence in their lives. They accept religion, love it, and appreciate it because of the rich blessings derived from it. . . . It becomes not a stimulus to service, but a substitute for it."[5]

I don't need to dwell on this struggle between the sinful and the holy natures within each of us—we're all painfully aware of it. But let's listen to Manford Gutzke once again as he clearly summarizes this issue for us:

> The Christian is involved in two contrary influences. The Spirit leads him into the will of God and the flesh leads him to do his own will. . . . The Christian . . . must deny himself and take up the cross and follow Christ. It will involve a critical struggle within the heart of the Christian. He will experience in his own small way some aspect of Gethsemane. . . . There will be times when to do the will of God will mean denying himself or something that is very real and very desirable. . . . If a person finds himself unwilling to yield, unwilling to do the will of God, it would be natural. One must deny himself again and again, daily. That requires the grace of God.[6]

And, we might add, it also requires the *strength* of God.

Finally, when struggling with opposition either from Satan or from our own sinful nature, we should always keep in mind God's promise in 1 Corinthians 10:13: "No temptation has overtaken you except such as is common to man; but God is faithful, who will not allow you to be tempted beyond what you are able, but with the temptation will also make the way of escape, that you may be able to bear it."

A third source of opposition is the one that might be most surprising to you. As you seek to serve God, not only will you be opposed by people who serve Satan and by your own sinful nature, but you will also encounter resistance from good people—even godly people—who misunderstand you. These are the people who you hope and expect would be most sympathetic and helpful to you, and yet you may occasionally find just the opposite to be true.

We saw in the last chapter that people have a natural desire for others to be like them, especially in matters of religion. We also saw that believers tend to emphasize those forms of service that utilize the gifts they themselves have. It is therefore naive to assume that your sincerity in serving God will protect you from the complaints of those who think you ought to serve God in a different way.

We don't have to look far to see Christians opposing the ministry of other believers because "that's not the way it's done." My opposition to my son Jim's ministry in Orlando is a perfect example of this. If he hadn't been serving in the strength of Christ and in the strength of knowing that God had clearly called him to that work, he might have been crushed; he might have quit the work; he might have missed God's calling on him at that time. And I would have been largely responsible. Thank God Jim was strong in the Lord and smarter than his dad!

Matthew 26 records the story of Jesus and His disciples visiting Simon the leper. As they were in Simon's house "a woman came to Him having an alabaster flask of very costly fragrant oil, and she poured it on His head as He sat at the table" (v. 7).

Here was a woman who was seeking to serve God and honor His Son, although in a way that we would find unusual today. "But when His disciples saw it, they were indignant, saying, 'To what purpose is this waste? For this fragrant oil might have been sold for much and given to the poor'" (vv. 8–9). Jesus' disciples were apparently well-intentioned, but they had a different idea of service than the woman had.

Jesus told His disciples, however, "Why do you trouble the woman? For she has done a good work for Me. . . . Assuredly, I say to you, wherever the gospel is preached in the whole world, what this woman has done will also be told as a memorial to her" (vv. 10, 13).

God's clear call to service includes His strength to carry out that service. And one reason we must rely on His strength is that we can be sure we'll face opposition as we carry out His call. This resistance will come from Satan, from our own sinful nature, and from other well-intentioned people who misunderstand what we're about.

Strength to Survive Prosperity

We think of God's strength as something we especially need when times are tough, when we're struggling with one thing after another and the whole world seems to be against us. When we read that Paul learned to lean on God in distress, peril, and extreme want, we understand immediately. That makes obvious sense to us. But living in God's strength is not a thing only for emergencies. It is an attitude—like praying without ceasing—that we must constantly cultivate in our lives.

What we who enjoy the affluence of the modern Western world must never forget is that being called by God means desperately needing His strength to survive *prosperity*, because that's when we're most easily tempted to abandon our servanthood. When we're poor, sick, or facing persecution or death, we have little trouble seeing that our strength isn't enough and that we need divine resources. But when things are going well, it's easy to forget God and think we've gotten all we need by ourselves.

When the children of Israel were about to enter the Promised Land after the Exodus from Egypt and forty years of wandering in the wilderness, the Lord knew they would be tempted to feel self-sufficient and ignore Him. So He warned them through Moses:

> When the Lord your God brings you into the land of which He swore to your fathers . . . to give you large and beautiful cities which you did not build, houses full of all good things, which you did not fill, hewn-out wells which you did not dig, vineyards and olive trees which you did not plant—when you have eaten and are full—then beware, lest you forget the Lord who brought you out of the land of Egypt from the house of bondage (Deut. 6:10–12).

Jesus sounded the same warning in the parable of the sower and the soils. "Some seed," He said, "fell among thorns; and the thorns grew up and choked it, and it yielded no crop." And who are these ones, these "seeds," who fell among the thorns? "They are the ones who hear the word, and the cares of this world, the deceitfulness of riches, and the desires for other things entering in choke the word, and it becomes unfruitful" (Mark 4:7, 18–19).

It is so easy to become comfortable, to grow to love money and things more than God, to seek the maintenance of our comfort more than the service of the Master. This is why Jesus said, "It is hard for a rich man to enter the kingdom of heaven" (Matt. 19:23).

For the same reason, Paul wrote to Timothy, "The love of money is a root of all kinds of evil, for which some have strayed from the faith in their greediness, and pierced themselves through with many sorrows" (1 Tim. 6:10).

Finally, it is why Jesus warned, "No one can serve two masters; for either he will hate the one and love the other, or else he will be loyal to the one and despise the other. You cannot serve God and mammon [money]" (Matt. 6:24).

Pastor and author Stephen Brown tells of talking with the crew of a television talk show after he had been the guest. The director of the show was very intense in his questioning and continued talking to Brown after everyone else had left.

Finally Brown realized he needed to leave in order to be on time for another appointment and said to the young man, "I have to leave, but let me write down on the back of my card the names of three or four books you ought to read. Read them and then let's get together for lunch and discuss them." He handed him the card and moved toward the door.

The director called after Brown, "Reverend, I don't believe I will read these books."

Brown turned to him and said, "What do you mean, you won't read the books? You were the one asking the questions, and those books might provide some of the answers."

With unusual honesty the young man replied, "If I read these books, I might find that all the things you have been saying to me are true. If they are true, then I'm going to have to change some of the things in my life, and I don't want to change."[7]

Here was a young man who had a good life as the world defines it, who was doing well and enjoying himself, and who didn't want to make any commitment that might involve giving some of that up. He was like many people in our world who are in grave spiritual danger because they have chosen the riches of this world over submission to God. He was just more honest than most.

Stephen Brown's story closely parallels one of the most tragic stories in the entire Bible, an incident out of the life of Jesus. A rich young ruler came to Jesus, apparently out of a genuine recognition of Jesus' authority and a sincere desire to be rightly related to God, and asked, "Good Teacher, what good thing shall I do that I may have eternal life?" The man was able to say confidently that he had kept the ten commandments since he was a boy, but he wanted to do something more.

Jesus recognized the potential in this young man, but He also knew that he loved his wealth more than he loved and wanted to serve God. So Jesus put him to the test and said, "If you want to be perfect, go, sell what you have and give to the poor, and you will have treasure in heaven; and come, follow Me."

The Bible then gives us the young ruler's response in these terrible words: "But when the young man heard that saying, he want away sorrowful, for he had great possessions."

Jesus' closing commentary on the incident was this warning: "Assuredly, I say to you that it is hard for a rich man to enter the kingdom of heaven" (see Matt. 19:16–26). That's not because God doesn't love the rich. Rather it is because prosperity can so easily draw our hearts away from God.

Remember, then, not to think of God's strength as something we need only in adversity. To the contrary, we are in greater spiritual danger—and therefore more in need of His strength—when we are enjoying prosperity.

Some clever person once said, "The Christian life isn't difficult; it's impossible!" However, that witty cliché tells only part of the story. For while it's true that in our own strength we can't be successful as servants, the fact of the matter is that God is fully aware of the problem, and He offers us His strength, which is more than sufficient.

As part of God's clear call to servanthood, He is calling you to serve in His strength, which He promises to make freely available. If you will depend upon Him, He will give you the might to serve as He leads, to overcome opposition, to stay true in prosperity as well as in adversity—to be the kind of powerful person whose life makes a difference.

---

1. David Seamands, *Healing for Damaged Emotions* (Wheaton: Victor, 1981), pp. 70–71.
2. Charles R. Swindoll, *Improving Your Serve*, p. 41.
3. Manford George Gutzke, *Born to Serve*, pp. 29–30, 33.
4. Ibid., p. 31.
5. Larry Maddox, "Called To Be Servants," *Church Training* (October, 1985), p. 14.
6. Gutzke, pp. 83–84.
7. Stephen Brown, *If God Is in Charge* (Nashville: Thomas Nelson, 1983), pp. 57–58.

Part II

A CLEAN
LIFE

GOD'S EXPECTATIONS
AND OUR EXCESSES

HE BUILT ONE OF THE country's largest independent Bible schools. In a few short years he was known and respected throughout America's evangelical community. He shared the dais with Christian leaders everywhere, speaking in the biggest churches and the most prestigious Christian institutions.

Then one day it was discovered that he had been sleeping with female students at the Bible school for some time. Not only that, but when the news got out, he left his wife and went away with the young woman who was his current lover.

Needless to say, this was a major scandal. The man's ministry was destroyed, his family was torn apart, non-Christians who heard about it had reason to discredit the church of Jesus Christ, and the reputation of the school was badly damaged as well. It went into a decline from which it has never fully recovered. All this happened because that one man refused to live a holy life and instead let his passions run out of control. Unfortunately, this is only one of many similar stories that could be told.

The Biblical Call to a Clean Life

When God ordained Jeremiah, He not only gave him a clear call to service, He also made it clear that He expected His servant to live a clean life: "Before you were born I sanctified you."

God's call to clean living resounds throughout the Bible, both the Old and New Testaments. It began with His instructions to Adam and Eve in the Garden of Eden not to eat the fruit of the tree of the knowledge of good and evil; it continued with His laws for the children of Israel, His "called-apart" people; and it is a prominent part of the teachings of Jesus and His apostles.

In Paul's great epistle to the Romans, he wrote, "I beseech you therefore, brethren, by the mercies of God, that you present your bodies a living sacrifice, holy, acceptable to God, which is your reasonable service" (12:1). That's about as clear as it can be, isn't it? (Someone has said that the problem with our being living sacrifices is that we keep trying to crawl down off the altar!)

The apostle Peter issued a call to holiness and also gave us the most important reason for it: "But as He who called you is holy, you also be holy in all your conduct, because it is written, 'Be holy, for I am holy'" (1 Peter 1:15–16). God wants us to be holy so that when people look at us, they will recognize that we are His children.

David expressed God's expectation that His servants lead a clean life this way in Psalm 24: "Who may ascend into the hill of the Lord? Or who may stand in His holy place? He who has clean hands and a pure heart, who has not lifted up his soul to an idol, nor sworn deceitfully" (vv. 3–4).

Paul said that the will of God is "your sanctification. . . . For God did not call us to uncleanness, but in holiness" (1 Thess. 4:3, 7). He further explained our call to a clean life in terms of slavery:

> Do not let sin control your puny body any longer; do not give in to its sinful desires. Do not let any part of your bodies become tools of wickedness, to be used for sinning; but give yourselves completely to God—every part of you—for you are back from death and you want to be tools in the hands of God, to be used for His good purposes. . . . Don't you realize that you can choose your own master? You can choose sin (with death) or else obedience (with acquittal). The one to whom you offer yourself—he will take you and be your master and you will be his slave. . . . I speak this way, using the illustration of slaves and masters, because it is easy to understand: just as you used to be slaves to all kinds of sin, so now you must let yourselves be slaves to all that is right and holy (Rom. 6:12-13, 16, 19, TLB).

Paul boldly reinforced that theme a short time later in the same letter to the Romans: "For if we live, we live to the Lord; and if we die, we die to the Lord. Therefore, whether we live or die, we are the Lord's" (14:8).

What Holiness Means

There can be no doubt that God calls His children to a clean and holy life. Having established that, however, we next need to understand what holiness is. Those verses above gave some idea, but we need to come to a basic, common understanding of this most important calling of God, for it's in living a holy life that we will know lasting joy.

Unfortunately, holiness most often gets defined in terms of a particular person's or group's list of acceptable and unacceptable behaviors—in a word, legalism. Now, holiness will indeed make a significant difference in the way we live. But at the most basic level—the one God cares about most—holiness is not a matter of actions but of heart and attitude. I explained in chapter 2 that servanthood is first a matter of commitment and attitude before the servant *does* anything, and the truth of holiness is exactly the same.

The people of Jesus' day, especially the religious leaders, had this all wrong. They had a detailed, complex list of rules and regulations governing all areas of their lives, and they believed that as long as they lived by those laws they could think as they pleased and take advantage of people in ways not specifically prohibited by their rules. Therefore, Jesus had some very harsh words for those leaders, the scribes and Pharisees: "Woe to you, scribes and Pharisees, hypocrites! For you cleanse the outside of the cup and dish, but inside they are full of extortion and self-indulgence. . . . Woe to you, scribes and Pharisees, hypocrites! For you are like whitewashed tombs which indeed appear beautiful outwardly, but inside are full of dead men's bones and all uncleanness" (Matt. 23:25, 27).

Those words are just a small sample of the many strong statements Jesus made in condemning people who lived outwardly clean lives but whose hearts were full of sin. They make it clear to us, though, that holiness has to begin inside us, where the real person lives. The problem is that people can follow a list of rules of behavior without ever loving and wanting to follow the Lord.

John Wesley, one of the great evangelists of the last few centuries, had to learn the truth that holiness is first an inward reality. During his college days at Oxford University, he belonged to the Holy Club, a group of young men who led lives of strict discipline according to the rules of the Church of England. They were known for their self-sacrifice, devotional practices, and charitable activities, all of which earned them the nickname of Methodists. After his ordination, Wesley came to the American colonies and did missionary work in Georgia before returning to England in 1738.

During all this time, however, as Wesley's journal later revealed, he had no joy in the Lord, and he even doubted whether he was really a Christian. This was because his concept of God-pleasing holiness was that God would accept Wesley "by my continued endeavour to keep his whole law, inward and outward." In a word, Wesley was a legalist. He thought *doing* the right things was all that really mattered, that he could earn God's favor by his actions. But, as Wesley found out, legalism does not bring joy; it brings either guilt or self-centered pride.

Then one day, as Wesley listened to the reading of Martin Luther's "Preface to the Book of Romans," he came to the realization that holiness means a changed heart first and foremost, and that out of such a heart comes true holy living. Wrote Wesley about this understanding that Christ's blood had saved him and made real holiness possible, "I felt my heart strangely warmed." It was then that Wesley began to know the joy of the Lord.

As Wesley discovered, legalism will never produce holiness because it is based on a misunderstanding of sin. It defines holiness in terms of behavior because it defines sin in terms of behavior. And as we've just seen, sin goes a lot deeper than our outward actions. Jesus made this point very clearly in the Sermon on the Mount when He said,

> You have heard that it was said to those of old, "You shall not murder," and whoever murders [an outward action] will be in danger of the judgment. But I say to you that whoever is angry with his brother without a cause [an inward attitude] shall be in danger of the judgment. . . . You have heard that it was said to those of old, "You shall not commit adultery" [an outward action]. But I say to you that whoever looks at a woman to lust for her [an inward attitude] has already committed adultery with her in his heart (Matt. 5:21–22, 27–28).

Before we consider what holiness means in our outward living, then, we must understand clearly that God looks on the heart first and foremost. If our lives are not clean there, then all the clean behavior in the world will not keep us in fellowship with our holy heavenly Father. If we have sinned in our hearts, it's the same in His eyes as if we'd actually done the thing about which we've thought. We must have holy hearts and minds if we're to be the servants God will use and bless with His peace and power. We will discuss the nuts and bolts of how we can pursue this inward holiness in the next chapter.

Holiness in Action

While holiness does not arise from keeping rules, we must also realize that true holiness *does* change the way we live. There should be evidence of the spiritual life that's in us for others to see. A servant must serve in some visible way; otherwise, the watching world has reason to wonder whether a person is in fact a servant.

You can tell if a person is alive physically by looking for vital signs. If a person is walking around and talking, it's a safe bet he's alive. If there's no movement, you'd check for a pulse or put a mirror in front of the mouth to see if there's any breath. As a last resort, you might attach a machine that measures brain activity. If there's any physical life, there will be some outward sign of it that you can measure, some sort of activity that indicates life is present.

The same principle holds true in the spiritual realm. James emphasized this when he said, "Faith by itself, if it does not have works, is dead. . . . For as the body without the spirit is dead, so faith without works is dead also" (James 2:17, 26). James was not disputing that we are saved from sin by faith. Rather, he was simply stating that if a person has been born again through faith in Christ, that person has new spiritual life. And if there's life, there will naturally be activity that all can recognize as a sign of the presence of life. If there is no such activity, there's probably no life.

Thus, while the holiness God seeks in His servants is first and foremost an inward reality, that reality should lead to some outward, visible patterns of living that the world will recognize as God-inspired and God-empowered. Jesus said, "Let your light so shine before men, that they may see your good works and glorify your Father in heaven" (Matt. 5:16).

Jesus was calling for His children to lead lives that are noticeably, visibly different from those of the people around us. When others see the difference in us and wonder about it, we'll be able to say that the reason is we're servants of the great God who is living in and empowering us. The most significant difference in those who are God's children is their love. Jesus said, "A new commandment I give to you, that you love one another; as I have loved you, that you also love one another. By this all will know that you are My disciples, *if you have love for one another*" (John 13:34-35, italics mine).

The outstanding characteristic of the children of God should be the quality of our love for one another and all those around us. This should be God's love, self-giving love, what is commonly known as *agape* love, which the apostle Paul described so eloquently in 1 Corinthians 13. John described one way such love is shown when he said, "But whoever has this world's goods, and sees his brother in need, and shuts up his heart from him, how does the love of God abide in him? My little children, let us not love in word or in tongue, but in deed and in truth" (1 John 3:17-18).

Holiness Today

So far in this chapter we've seen that God expects His children to be holy, that holiness is primarily a matter of heart and commitment, but that holiness should also be manifested in the way we live, especially the way we love. We've seen, too, that there are problems with legalism, the making of lists of behaviors by which we judge our own holiness as well as that of others. Having said that, however, we need to consider how else (besides love) holiness might be seen in our daily lives.

The main point of holiness is that, as the apostle Paul said, we are no longer our own. God bought us at the cost of His Son, and we are now set apart as His. We have the opportunity to fellowship with Him, to grow in our knowledge of Him, to serve in His cause, and to gradually become more and more like Him as we spend time in His presence. In this sense, holiness is a very positive, joyful thing. Holiness means purity, of course—the way in which it's usually understood—but it's really much more than that. Holiness is a motivation that should touch every area of our lives.

The goal of holiness is to conform us to God's image, and the first part of life this will affect is our use of time. If there were a person who lived near you and whom you greatly admired, how would you go about getting to know him better and emulating his good qualities? Would you ignore him, deliberately passing up opportunities to spend time with him, turning down his invitations to get together for a visit? If he sent you letters of encouragement and instruction, would you put them on a shelf and leave them there unopened? Of course not!

The key to knowing and becoming more like anyone is to spend time with him—there's just no substitute. And this is true of our relationship with God as well. When I came to this realization many years ago, it revolutionized my use of time, especially my devotional time. I hope it will do the same for yours.

A daily quiet time is often discussed in Christian circles, and it is a practice we're all admonished to adopt as a habit. I suspect it's also a source of much guilt, because I'm sure the great majority of Christians have not developed such a habit. Why? Primarily because most people see it as a chore, a duty, something that's supposed to be good for you—like broccoli—but that's no fun at all. If most Christians have a quiet time, it's only because they feel they ought to, not because they want to.

But think of it this way: Do you admire God? Do you love Him? Do you believe He loves you? Do you think He's a source of wisdom? comfort? strength? Does He have some qualities you would like to see in your own life? Would you like to know the Creator-God better? If your answer to one or more of these questions is yes, do you begin to see what a wonderful opportunity a daily devotional time is?

I tell you in all honesty, there is no more exciting time in my life day after day than the time I spend reading God's Word and talking with Him. I wouldn't miss it for anything. It's not something I do only out of a sense of obligation or to avoid guilt, but the best, most profitable use of time I can imagine. This doesn't mean that I always get goose bumps, but I know that as I regularly spend time with the Lord, He's teaching me, guiding me, and molding me into His likeness. That's exciting! I also leave that time each morning with the renewed assurance that whatever I face that day, my great and loving God will be there with me.

Holiness affects our use of time, especially the priority we give each day to time alone with the Father. And as we spend time with Him and maintain an attitude of wanting to become more like Him, He gradually works a transformation in our hearts and lives so that we are changed. We can't make this change happen for ourselves, but God can and will do it if we let Him.

Such a transformation growing out of regularly being with the Lord will have noticeable effects throughout our lives. For example, if you have struggled with a foul mouth, you'll find your speech coming under control. If you have developed a reputation for dishonesty, people will notice you are becoming more trustworthy. If you have been known to be generally unsympathetic toward others, people will see that you're starting to have a warm and genuine concern for them. Indeed, as we grow in God, there is not an area of our lives where we won't see ourselves becoming more like Him. That transformation is what holiness is all about, and it begins when we want to be with God and to grow to be like Him more than we want the things—whatever they may be— that keep us away from His presence.

When we approach holiness from this perspective, we can see that we don't need a list of six steps toward spiritual maturity, four keys to cleaning up our language, or any other such list. The fact is that only God can work such changes deep in our inner being, and this He will do as we draw close to Him and give Him the freedom to work in our lives.

Another way to understand this and to know what a holy life looks like is to consider Galatians 5, where Paul lists some of the qualities God will develop in us as part of the "fruit of the Spirit." There we see that the person who is becoming like his Lord will live in "love, joy, peace, longsuffering, kindness, goodness, faithfulness, gentleness, self-control" (Gal. 5:22–23). These will grow naturally out of a heart set apart to God.

The Danger of Pride, the Value of Humility

There is one sin in particular that is totally opposed to the development of holiness in us, and we need to be especially alert to its presence in our lives. That sin is pride, the first sin of Satan when he wanted to "exalt my throne above the stars of God . . . [and] be like the Most High" (Isa. 14:13–14). It is so dangerous because the person ruled by pride is not interested in being set apart for God, drawing near to Him, and being changed into His likeness. Instead, the proud person feels he has no need of God and is unwilling to submit to His authority. He rejects the idea that God has any reason to transform him in any way.

Pride is also another of the great dangers of legalism. It seems those who define holiness in terms of whether one follows lists of rules or not tend to think themselves much better than those who do not subscribe to such a list. To this kind of pride Paul said, "For I say, through the grace given to me, to everyone who is among you, not to think of himself more highly than he ought to think, but to think soberly, as God has dealt to each one a measure of faith" (Rom. 12:3).

The Book of Proverbs contains many warnings against pride and affirmations of humility. Here are just a few: "Pride goes before destruction, and a haughty spirit before a fall" (16:18). "When pride comes, then comes shame; but with the humble is wisdom" (11:2). "A man's pride will bring him low, but the humble in spirit will retain honor" (29:23).

The apostle Peter gave a similar caution: "Be clothed with humility, for 'God resists the proud, but gives grace to the humble.' Therefore humble yourselves under the mighty hand of God, that He may exalt you in due time" (1 Peter 5:5–6).

When we are proud, we think more highly of ourselves than we should. If we're tempted by pride, we need to remember that we were lost sinners without hope before God acted on our behalf to make salvation possible, and that we're still sinners today. When we committed ourselves to Jesus as our Savior and Lord, we didn't become perfect or even a lot better than other people. We are just forgiven, and that was all God's doing.

As Charles Swindoll points out, however, a true spirit of humility is hard to find these days: "This spirit of humility is very rare in our day of strong-willed, proud-as-a-peacock attitudes. The clenched fist has replaced the bowed head. The big mouth and the surly stare now dominate the scene once occupied by the quiet godliness of the 'poor in spirit.' How self-righteous we have become! How confident in and of ourselves!"[1]

Because pride is so dangerous, so deadly, so contrary to God's will, a cardinal virtue of the servant is humility. Manford Gutzke shows us how service and humility are related: "The greatest qualification one could ever have to serve God is to know that one is not fit—no self-defense, no explanation, no alibis, no excuses, no promises to do better—just a humble, honest, repentant confession, 'I am not worthy.'"[2]

Unfortunately, there are many people active in church work not because they are committed to serving God, but because they love the recognition they receive and the way it feeds their pride. If you recognize that some of your own efforts have been motivated by pride, I encourage you to try this remedy suggested by Richard Foster:

> Nothing *transforms* the desires of the flesh like serving in hiddenness. The flesh whines against service but screams against hidden service. It strains and pulls for honor and recognition. It will devise subtle, religiously acceptable means to call attention to the service rendered. If we stoutly refuse to give in to this lust of the flesh we crucify it. Every time we crucify the flesh, we crucify our pride and arrogance.[3]

Secret service is undoubtedly the best kind, where only God and His servant know who has done the faithful deed. Many types of service do not lend themselves to being hidden, of course, such as when Billy Graham speaks before a crowd of fifty thousand and an additional television audience of millions. Still, hidden service has great value precisely because it leaves no room for pride.

The attitude toward which we should strive is summarized well by Swindoll: "Instead of keeping a record of what we've done or who we've helped, we'll take delight in forgetting the deed(s) and being virtually unnoticed. Our hunger for public recognition will diminish in significance."[4]

Finally, what are some of the benefits that come to us when we're truly humble? Let me offer just two as suggested by two outstanding writers of the recent past. The first comes from A. W. Tozer, who echoed 1 Peter 5:6 concerning the results of humbling ourselves before God:

> Let no one imagine that he will lose anything of human dignity by this voluntary sell-out of his all to his God. He does not by this degrade himself as a man; rather he finds his right place of high honor as one made in the image of his Creator. His deep disgrace lay in his moral derangement, his unnatural usurpation of the place of God. His honor will be proved by restoring again the stolen throne. In exalting God over all, he finds his own highest honor upheld.[5]

In other words, when we honor God by submitting to Him in humility, He honors us for our obedience.

We see another benefit of humility in the writing of Thomas Kelly, who pointed out that when we submit ourselves humbly to the Lord, we are able to enjoy a unique boldness in our service that makes life exciting and fulfilling.

> There is something about deepest humility which makes men bold. For utter obedience is self-forgetful obedience. No longer do we hesitate and shuffle and apologize because, say we, we are weak, lowly creatures and the world is a pack of snarling wolves among whom we are sent as sheep by the Shepherd. . . . If we live in complete humility in God we can smile in patient assurance as we work. Will you be wise enough and humble enough to be little fools of God? For who can finally stay His power?[6]

You and I have the responsibility ourselves to be humble. Nowhere in Scripture does it say for us to pray for humility. Rather, it tells us to humble ourselves: "He who humbles himself will be exalted" (Luke 14:11, 18:14). This is the job of the Christian. The Scripture also says, "If My people who are called by My name will humble themselves, and pray and seek My face, and turn from their wicked ways, then I will hear from heaven, and will forgive their sin and heal their land" (2 Chron. 7:14).

No Hypocrites Either, If You Please

In addition to humility, God is looking for consistency in holy lives. He wants us to live as though we believe what we say about our love for and desire to serve Him. We are to "be doers of the word, and not hearers only" (James 1:22).

Think of what it can mean if our lives are consistent with our words, if we show by our actions the same love that we claim is part of the very nature of the Lord! We can tell people how wonderful God and the Christian life are, but unless our lives back up those statements, people won't believe us—and they shouldn't.

If we strive, however, to live consistently with our message, and if we're honest with people about the struggles along the way, our heavenly Father will be pleased. As Charles Swindoll says, "God desires his servants to be 'real' people—authentic to the core."[7] And if they are? "Christ promises that consistent servants who are pure in heart 'shall see God.' There is no doubt about the destiny of these individuals. For sure, some glorious day in the future, these servants will see the Lord and hear the most significant words that will ever enter human ears: 'Well done, good and faithful slave; you were faithful . . . enter into the joy of your master' (Matt. 25:21)."[8]

Our Excesses

We've examined at some length the clean, holy life God expects of His servants. It's an awesome calling, isn't it? It looks pretty tough to live up to those standards, doesn't it? The fact is that on this side of eternity we will never reach perfection. In heaven, the struggle with sin and self will finally be over, and what a wonderful hope that is. But in the meantime, the fight goes on.

Even for the most faithful followers of God, there is a constant battle to love God more than the pleasure of sin and to trust Him more than one's own resources. Indeed, I think God's greatest saints have the greatest struggles because Satan wants to blunt their effectiveness and so continually throws temptations to sin in their paths. And because of the sinful nature that we all still carry around, even the best are going to fall into sin from time to time. But for the child of God, lasting joy will come in winning the battle for holiness in his life—a victory that God wants him to win.

Remember David, that great king of Israel? He so loved and worshiped the Lord that he was identified in the Bible as "a man after God's own heart." When you read the psalms he wrote, you begin to appreciate how great was David's trust in God. He is a genuine hero of the Bible. And yet this man of enormous faith failed God utterly when faced with the temptation of seeing Bathsheba, another man's wife, as she was bathing.

Watching Bathsheba, David lusted after her and used his royal authority to have her brought to himself so he could commit adultery with her. As if that weren't bad enough, he then had her husband killed in an attempt to cover up what he had done. After the man, Uriah, was dead, David took Bathsheba for his wife.

When David was confronted with his sins by the prophet Nathan, he confessed and repented, giving us a good example of how we should respond to our own sins (see Ps. 51). But the fact is that this great man of faith had fallen into adultery, deceit, murder, sinful manipulation of others, and probably many other sins as well for the better part of a year before being called to account by the prophet of God. David's joy did not come in sinning—even though we might think that it should have if we believe the picture of life painted by television, movies, and novels today. Rather, his joy came in repentance and getting right with God. If such a man could fall so far from God's holiness, we should not be surprised that we also fail.

The apostle Paul painted a grim picture of humanity's sinful nature in the first chapter of his letter to the Roman Christians. He had to warn them in that same letter, "Do not let sin reign in your mortal body, that you should obey it in its lusts. And do not present your members as instruments of unrighteousness to sin, but present yourselves to God . . . and your members as instruments of righteousness to God" (Rom. 6:12–13). Clearly, they were struggling to live holy lives, even as we do today.

Of his own inner conflict Paul wrote, "I know I am rotten through and through so far as my old sinful nature is concerned. No matter which way I turn I can't make myself do right. I want to but I can't. When I want to do good, I don't; and when I try not to do wrong, I do it anyway" (Rom. 7:18–19, TLB). Even the great apostle Paul, who described himself repeatedly and sincerely as a willing slave of Christ, had to struggle daily to live in holiness, and many times he failed, as we all do.

I review all this to impress upon you the reality that while we live on this earth, even after we've committed our lives to the Lord, to be His servants and live holy lives, we are going to fail. We will sin from time to time. Perhaps our sins won't hurt others or get a lot of publicity like those of King David or that Bible college president I mentioned at the beginning of this chapter. But that doesn't make our offenses any less serious in the sight of God.

When we see a poor person walk by us on the street and we know something of what it means to struggle financially, we sometimes say, "There but for the grace of God go I." When you see someone disgraced after his sin is revealed in public, you should say the same thing. When someone is caught in a lie he has told, are you reminded of the "little white lies" you've told that supposedly didn't hurt anybody and that have never been found out? In God's eyes, the two sins are the same. When a murderer is convicted, do you think of the private hates you've entertained? There's no difference between the two offenses before the Lord.

God has called us to a clean and holy life. The bad news is that because of the sinful nature that's still within us, we'll sometimes falter in following Him as we give in to the temptations of Satan and the world. The good news, however, is that we're not left alone to struggle with these things. We have the real hope of growth and increasing victory as God gives us His strength and many other resources for effective service that brings lasting joy.

---

1. Charles R. Swindoll, *Improving Your Serve*, p. 101.
2. Manford George Gutzke, *Born to Serve*, p. 47.
3. Richard Foster, *Celebration of Discipline*, pp. 113–14.
4. Swindoll, p. 42.
5. A.W. Tozer, *A Treasury of A.W. Tozer* (Grand Rapids: Baker, 1980), p. 108.
6. Thomas R. Kelly, *A Testament of Devotion* (New York: Harper & Row, 1941), pp. 108–9.
7. Swindoll, p. 114.
8. Ibid., pp. 115–16.

THE KEYS TO
A HOLY LIFE

I HOPE YOU KNOW at least one person who seems set apart for God and lives a holy life. God expects His children to lead increasingly clean and holy lives and one of the best ways to see how to do this is through the examples of others. Billy Graham comes as close as anyone I know to living a holy life. Mother Teresa of Calcutta also comes to mind—that marvelous lady who has dedicated her life to offering comfort and love to the world's dying outcasts in the name of the Lord.

Another great man of God who was truly set apart for Him was a simple French monk, a kitchen worker in the monastery where he lived and worshiped. Born Nicholas Herman, he became known simply as Brother Lawrence, and you can get to know him through the writings he left behind.

The legacy of Brother Lawrence is the result of a close and continual walk with God. Over the course of several years, he developed the habit of feeling himself to be always in the presence of God, of carrying on an unending conversation with the Father regardless of what else he was doing. The result of this "practice of the presence of God" was a deep knowledge of and faith in God, a life motivated by love, a heart filled with sincere humility.

Brother Lawrence's counsel to us is that "we should feed our soul with a lofty conception of God and from that derive great joy in being his."[1] When Brother Lawrence did some good deed, he would speak to the Lord and say, "God, I should not be able to do that unless you enabled me to do it."[2] And when he sinned, he would confess it to God and say to Him, "I should never do anything else if you left it to me to do it."[3]

Truly this was a man who knew God, who dedicated his life to Him and walked closely with Him day by day, who lived with consistency and humility, providing us with a shining example.

But practically speaking, how do we lead a clean and holy life? The Bible is clear about what God wants, but what can we do to make such a life a daily reality instead of just so much "pie in the sky"?

Bob Cook, a Christian educator and veteran radio broadcaster, summarized the answer exceptionally well:

> Human character, decisions and destiny all grow out of thought. What you think determines what you are, and what you will become. "As he thinketh in his heart, so is he," Solomon remarked. Godless character grows out of excluding God from one's thoughts: "God is not in all his thoughts," said the psalmist. Godly character comes from including your Lord and His attributes in your thinking: "Whatever things are true . . . honest . . . just . . . lovely, *think on these things*."[4]

In that simple but profound statement, you have the key to holy living in a nutshell. The struggle for a clean, God-honoring life is waged in the mind.

The Importance of Our Minds

What we are and what we do begins in our minds. Dr. Cook went on to say,

> All of us have small slices of time when we are free to think about anything we please. It is at these points that particular attention needs to be paid to monitoring and controlling your thoughts . . . your daydreams, if you will. What you think about when you don't *have* to think about anything in particular exerts a powerful influence on your destiny! Let your fantasies proceed unchecked and undisciplined, and they will inevitably produce undisciplined conduct. You are what you think.[5]

This recognition that what we are and do originates in our thoughts led someone to write this familiar line years ago: Sow a thought, reap an action. Sow an action, reap a habit. Sow a habit, reap a life.

People who work with computers put the same idea in the acronym G.I.G.O., which means "garbage in, garbage out." The principle is that if you feed the wrong information into a computer, you shouldn't expect to get anything out of it but wrong information. Likewise, if we repeatedly feed garbage into our minds, we should expect to get garbage back in the form of our words and attitudes and actions.

This truth is why the apostle James described in the following way how sinful activity comes about: "Each one is tempted when he is drawn away by his own desires [sinful thoughts] and enticed. Then, when desire has conceived, it gives birth to sin" (James 1:14–15). Sin begins in the mind, the thoughts and desires.

Likewise, this is why in Matthew 5 Jesus equated sinful thoughts and sinful actions. In reality they are the same. An action is just an extension of the thoughts that preceded it. Jesus spoke in the same vein when He condemned the hypocrisy of the Pharisees in Matthew 15. Those religious leaders faithfully kept their list of legalistic rules—such as washing their hands in a carefully prescribed manner before eating—but their hearts, their minds, and their desires were full of sin. So Jesus said of them to His disciples,

Do you not yet understand that whatever enters the mouth goes into
the stomach and is eliminated? But those things which proceed out
of the mouth come from the heart, and they defile a man. For out of
the heart proceed evil thoughts, murders, adulteries, fornications,
thefts, false witness, blasphemies. These are the things which defile
a man, but to eat with unwashed hands does not defile a man (Matt.
5:17–20).

And how were these thought patterns revealed in the lives of
the Pharisees? For one thing, they were known to dishonor their
parents under the guise of upholding their law, an action motivated by covetousness (see Matt. 15:7–9). Moreover, Jesus seems
to be saying in the statement above that the Pharisees were guilty
of *all* the things He listed. And lest you think that's too extreme
a judgment, remember that it was the Pharisees who were so full
of hatred and murder that they plotted to have Jesus unjustly
crucified.

Controlling Our Minds for Holy Living

Our thoughts are the ground from which our lives grow. We are
what we think. Therefore, holy living begins by controlling our
thoughts, by thinking holy thoughts rather than sinful thoughts.
Using Dr. Cook's terms, we might say that the key to holy living is
to discipline our fantasies. This is in keeping with the principle
discussed in chapter 5 that holiness must first of all be an inward
reality and then holy living can grow out of it. And holy living
produces joy—lasting joy.

Now, you may be thinking that all I've said sounds good but
terribly idealistic and impractical, if not downright impossible.
How *do* we actually go about controlling our minds and thoughts
so that we're growing progressively more holy? That's exactly
what I want to try to show you in the remainder of this chapter
and the next.

Begin by evaluating what you're routinely allowing into your
mind now. Think back over how you've spent your free time the
last few nights. Do you come home from work worn out and

tired, and plop down in front of the television for the rest of the evening? It should go without saying that that's not the best use of your time, but if you're a typical American, the fact is you probably spend a lot of time watching television.

If you do, what are you watching? Are they shows that glamorize and glorify violence, extramarital sex, and materialistic greed? A large percentage of prime-time network programming does just that. And if that's what you watch much of the time, should it be any surprise that you find yourself thinking sinful thoughts in idle moments?

Remember, garbage in, garbage out. Take stock every few weeks of how you spend your spare time. Keep a log for a few days at a stretch so that you can get an accurate picture of the kinds of things you allow into your mind—television shows watched, books and magazine articles read, music listened to, and so on. If you find that much of it is material that is likely to have a negative effect on your efforts to live a holy life, it's time to make some changes—not because God is an ogre who doesn't want you to have any fun, but because you love Him and want to please Him, and because you are learning that unbroken fellowship with Him is the greatest and most lasting joy of all.

When you've evaluated what kind of ideas and thoughts you've been allowing into your mind, you should begin using the resources God has provided to help you live the life to which He has called you. Although there are many such resources, I want to focus on five of the main ones that we simply can't ignore. These are the keys to a holy life.

The Holy Spirit: The Christian's attempt to live a holy life must begin with the Holy Spirit, the third Person of the Godhead, who comes to indwell each believer at the moment of conversion.

How does the Holy Spirit help us with clean living? First, He is our source of strength from God, the strength we desperately need, as we saw in chapter 4. Jesus said just before His ascension into heaven, "You shall receive power when the Holy Spirit has come upon you" (Acts 1:8). And the scriptural account of the Day of Pentecost and the events that followed it (see Acts 2) shows that the indwelling Holy Spirit is indeed a source of supernatural power.

Paul also made it clear that the Spirit is the power source for our victory over sin: "If you keep on following it [your sinful nature] you are lost and will perish, but if *through the power of the Holy Spirit* you crush it and its evil deeds, you shall live" (Rom. 8:13, TLB, italics mine).

Believe me, if you attempt to live a holy life and control your thoughts by relying only on your own strength, you are doomed to frustration and failure. You need the power of the Holy Spirit working in and through you.

The Spirit also guides us in discerning between truth and lies, good and bad, better and best. Jesus said of Him, "When He, the Spirit of truth, has come, He will guide you into all truth" (John 16:13). Satan is the father of lies, and he and those who work with him (knowingly or not) are always trying to deceive God's people to make them fall into sin. Thus, we would be in grave trouble if we did not have the Spirit to help us see the truth.

Next, the Holy Spirit teaches us the things of God and His Word, imparts the knowledge we need to channel our thoughts in the right direction, and grants us the wisdom in making right decisions. Again, Jesus said of Him, "The Helper, the Holy Spirit, whom the Father will send in My name, He will teach you all things, and bring to your remembrance all things that I said to you" (John 14:26).

The apostle Paul expressed the Spirit's teaching ministry this way: "For what man knows the things of a man except the spirit of the man which is in him? Even so no one knows the things of God except the Spirit of God. Now we have received, not the spirit of the world, but the Spirit who is from God, that we might know the things that have been freely given to us by God" (1 Cor. 2:11–12).

The power of the Holy Spirit is essential for living a holy life. To let Him control your life, begin each day by committing your-self in prayer to God the Spirit. Ask Him to guide you through-out the day as you go about your business and relate to various people. Ask Him to strengthen you in times of temptation so you can stand firm against it, to remind you of the truths of God's Word when you need them, to guard your thoughts from straying into sinful areas, to develop His fruit in your life, to draw you ever closer to the Father and to make you ever more willing to be transformed into His image. Then, during the day, when you need wisdom or strength, remember that He is only a prayer away. Call on Him and He will never disappoint you.

The Bible: The G.I.G.O. principle emphasizes the importance of keeping intellectual and spiritual garbage out of your mind, but that's only half the story of holy living. You see, it's not enough that you keep garbage out. Your mind is always active, always working. It is never empty of thought. If you doubt that, take a minute and try to clear your mind completely so that it's entirely blank. You can't do it! Thus, controlling your thoughts for holy living means not only keeping garbage out, but also replacing it with good, God-honoring thoughts. And this is where God's Word, the Bible, becomes vital.

In the quotation at the beginning of this chapter, Bob Cook cited part of Philippians 4:8, but it bears repeating in its entirety: "Finally, brethren, whatever things are true, whatever things are noble, whatever things are just, whatever things are pure, whatever things are lovely, whatever things are of good report, if there is any virtue and if there is anything praiseworthy—meditate on these things." Now, I ask you, isn't that list a good description of God's Word?

The point is that to control your thoughts for holy living you must not only put garbage out of your mind, but you must fill it with the Word of God, thus giving your mind something good to dwell on and provide godly motivation for what you say and do. The psalmist said, "How can a young man cleanse his way? By taking heed according to Your word. . . . Your word I have hidden in my heart, that I might not sin against You" (Ps. 119:9, 11).

Dr. Cook also said, "Fill the niches and corners of every day with portions of the Word of God. . . . The unconscious mind is like a great computer; and what you program into it will be faithfully cranked out under pressure. Program portions of the Word of God into the computer of your mind."[6]

"Hiding God's Word in your heart" and "programming the Word of God into the computer of your mind" are different ways of saying that we need to read, study, memorize, and meditate upon the Bible until our minds are saturated with it. We must know what the Word says, we must plant the actual words in our minds, and we must contemplate their meaning and their message in our lives.

I know that reading the Bible can be difficult, especially if you haven't yet made a habit of it. And you may not know how to go about Bible study. You may also think memorizing is for children and meditation is for Eastern mystics. But I assure you that filling your mind with God's Word through these means is vital for believers of all ages.

Let me suggest just a few ways you can build the Bible into your life. First, it's a good practice to read through the entire Bible in a year's time. There are many plans that can guide you in doing this. You'll find them in many study Bibles or you can get one from your pastor or a Christian bookstore.

Most Bible reading plans simply divide the Bible into 365 segments, starting with Genesis and going through Revelation. Some divide a day's reading into morning and evening segments, the early portion usually being from the New Testament and the later from the Old (since the Old Testament is more than twice as long as the New, this segment will be longer, and you presumably have more time for reading in the evening than you do in the morning). Try several different plans for a few days to see which approach you prefer. Then incorporate one into your daily devotional time.

The advantage of such a read-through-in-a-year plan is that it gives you a good overview of the entire Bible and how it all fits together. You don't just read a few favorite passages over and over while ignoring the rest of the Book. The drawback, however, is that you don't get to know any one passage very well. Therefore, you might want to try a couple of other approaches to Bible reading as well.

One method is to read through the books of Proverbs and Psalms each month, a practice Billy Graham has followed for many years. Proverbs is a book of great practical wisdom and it has thirty-one chapters. Thus, if you read one chapter each day, you will have read it through in a month. The book of Psalms, on the other hand, leads our hearts and minds into marvelous worship of God, and it deepens our faith in Him. It has been a favorite of many believers through the years. If you read five of its one hundred and fifty chapters each day, you can go through it in a month also. This is the way Billy reads through these two wonderful books each month.

A second method I highly recommend is to take a portion of the Bible that can be read in about twenty minutes at a normal reading speed and read it through every day for a month. In the New Testament, this means a portion of about seven chapters or less. You might, for example, read the entire book of Colossians every day—it's only four chapters, but it's an excellent place to start because of its emphasis on the person and work of Jesus Christ. Most of the New Testament epistles can be read through every day in this time frame. A longer book such as the Gospel of John could be divided into segments: read the first seven chapters through each day for a month, the next seven for the next month, and the last seven for the third month.

The advantage of this method is that at the end of a month's reading, you will know those seven or so chapters extremely well and you will have planted that portion of God's Word deep in your mind, where God can cause it to bear much fruit.

Whatever method you use, read while your mind is fresh, and read expectantly. Even on days when you don't think you are learning anything, you are putting God's Word into your mind, and God has promised that it will always be effective (see Isa. 55:11).

Bible memorization is also important. I suggest you learn one or at most two verses a week. Write out your memory verses on an index card that you can carry in your purse or pocket so that you can review them frequently. Learn each verse a phrase at a time. Then string the phrases together. Your mind has a huge capacity for such memorization, but it may be difficult at first, so be patient with yourself, and keep working at it.

What verses should you memorize? I strongly recommend the

Topical Memory System published by the Navigators and available through any Christian bookstore. It organizes helpful verses topically, and it includes preprinted cards and a packet for carrying them. You can also choose verses from your Bible reading that you find particularly helpful. Or you can choose verses that meet some special need. If you have trouble trusting God, for example, you would do well to memorize Psalm 23 and recite it often in your mind.

Finally, you should meditate on God's Word. Let me recommend two resources to you: a booklet titled *Meditation*, written by Jim Downing and published by NavPress; and chapter 2 in Richard Foster's fine book *Celebration of Discipline*. The benefits of Scripture meditation are well worth pursuing: It offers a deeper understanding of the Bible, the opportunity to hear God speak to you in a very personal way through a given Scripture passage, and a wonderful sense of being in God's presence as you let your mind dwell on His words.

Keep in mind as you get deeply involved in the Bible that your lazy, sinful nature will rebel against your becoming serious about God's Word. Don't give in to it! Filling your mind with God's thoughts is too important. Ask for His strength, and force yourself to do it. Then, when you need help in your daily living, God will bring those portions of His Word that you've learned to your mind at just the time you need them most.

Let me say it again because it's so important: It is not enough to keep garbage out of your mind. You must fill your mind with good, God-honoring thoughts, and that primarily means filling your mind with the Word of God. As it permeates your thinking, you will fulfill the command of God through the apostle Paul, "Do not be conformed to this world, but *be transformed by the renewing of your mind*, that you may prove what is that good and acceptable and perfect will of God" (Rom. 12:2, italics mine).

Prayer: A third resource, or key, God gives to help us control our minds is prayer. It is in prayer that we ask God to empower us through the Spirit. And we're encouraged to pray about whatever concerns us (see Phil. 4:6), especially when we need wisdom in trying to be holy in the face of trials and temptations (see James 1:5). But prayer needs to be more than calling out to God when we're in trouble. It needs to become an ongoing conversation that we enjoy with our heavenly Father throughout the day, every day.

Paul expressed this simply when he said, "Pray without ceasing" (1 Thess. 5:17). Now, obviously you can't be on your knees twenty-four hours a day, nor can you keep your eyes closed all the time. If you ever choose to try that, please don't drive on the same road I'm on! But you can keep your mind open to the Lord all the time, and you can converse with Him in moments when your mind is free. Among other things, you can ask Him to help you understand and apply those portions of Scripture you're learning.

Once again, Bob Cook offers words of wisdom, this time on the type of prayer about which I'm talking:

> Make the Lord Jesus Christ lord of your mind. This takes more than a routine "bless me!" kind of prayer. "Bringing into captivity every thought," says Paul, "to the obedience of Christ." This concept demands willingness to engage in a life-long surrender of the thought process to your Lord . . . moment by moment. . . . Pray about everything in your schedule so that God can make you think about things as you should. . . . Let us learn to pray about daily tasks as a means of bringing our thoughts into line with God's.[7]

To pray without ceasing will mold your thoughts so that they are more and more in line with God's. This will help your mind to become holy. When we consistently turn our thoughts to God in prayer, seeking His fellowship, love, strength, and wisdom, we will find that our thoughts are gradually purified and under control. To learn more about this kind of prayer, I would heartily recommend you read Brother Lawrence's classic *Practicing the Presence of God.*

This matter of turning your mind toward God in prayer can be developed into a habit just like any good habit—with time and repetition. Include this desire in your morning prayer of commitment, and then, with the Spirit's help, make a conscious effort to go to the Lord throughout each day with your concerns and needs, intercessions for others, praise and thanksgiving. Nothing that matters to you is too small to be of interest to our loving heavenly Father.

Fellowship: The fourth resource God gives us for holy living is fellowship with other Christians. Solomon said wisely, "As iron sharpens iron, so a man sharpens the countenance of his friend" (Prov. 27:17). As you meet with other believers to discuss your experiences and the lessons you've learned, you can strengthen and encourage one another in the pursuit of holiness. Two believers helping each other are much stronger than two struggling to make it alone.

When attempting to live a holy life, it is very helpful to have someone to whom you're accountable, someone with whom you meet regularly and who you know is going to ask how things are going. The same is true when you try anything difficult. Perhaps you've tried to diet or begin an exercise program by yourself and found it extremely hard. If so, you're a typical human being. It's not easy to discipline yourself to form new and good habits, especially on your own. That's why it's helpful to team up with a fellow dieter or exerciser and check in with each other occasionally. Knowing that Joe or Susan is going to call you Friday and ask about your weight gives you extra incentive to turn down that tantalizing piece of chocolate cake that's making your mouth water.

Likewise in the Christian life, being accountable to another believer can help you discipline yourself. If Joe or Sue is going to call on Friday and ask how your Scripture reading and memorization are going, you're more likely to do the work you've agreed to than if you didn't expect such a call. It's just human nature, and part of how we can help each other in the pursuit of holiness.

There's another reason why Christian fellowship is important to us. Just as our minds are influenced by what we watch, read, and hear, they are also deeply affected by those with whom we spend the most time. We tend to become like people we are with. This is why children are so much like their parents in many ways, often without realizing it. Similarly, husbands and wives who have been married a long time tend to look, sound, and act like each other in many ways.

God has called His children to go into the world and tell sinners of His gospel of reconciliation through the blood of Christ, and that means spending time with non-Christians. But it is also vital that we spend time with fellow Christians so that we may observe and absorb the holiness in their lives. We need their examples, just as they need ours.

The importance of fellowship is part of why I consider myself one of the most fortunate men alive. For many years I have lived and worked and prayed and worshiped closely with men like Billy Graham, Cliff Barrows, George Beverly Shea, and my brother Grady. The lessons I have learned from them and the examples I have seen in them are priceless. I thank God that in some small ways I have become like these great servants of His because of my long association with them.

When you meet with another Christian or group of believers for this kind of fellowship, there must be an agreement of trust and confidentiality because you need to give honest reports of how your spiritual lives have been going in the last week. You might talk about helpful truths God has been teaching you. You could help each other with Scripture memory. You should certainly encourage and pray for one another, perhaps covenanting to pray about some specific concern of your partner's every day for a month, expecting God to provide some clear answer by the end of that time.

If you are not already part of such an active fellowship that helps you in your pursuit of holiness, I would encourage you to seek one out. Perhaps opportunities exist in your church, or perhaps there is a neighborhood Bible study where this kind of fellowship is available. Maybe a mature Christian friend will agree to meet with you regularly and help you. Wherever you can find the fellowship you need, make it a point to become involved and you will see real progress in your Christian walk.

Purposing in Your Heart: The last key to holy living I want to talk about is to purpose in your heart how you will respond to temptation before it comes. You know that you will be tempted to sin in the future and you should make up your mind now how you are going to react before temptation comes. This will give you a much greater chance of resisting it successfully.

The Bible gives us a marvelous example of this principle at work in the book of Daniel. The nation of Israel had been conquered by Babylon, and King Nebuchadnezzar had ordered that some of the most outstanding young men of Israel, including Daniel and three of his friends, be brought to his palace for training so that they could serve him in his court.

Now, the king wanted these young men to play an important part in the administration of his empire, and so he treated them well while they went through their three-year course in Babylonian language and literature. He gave them food and wine from his own kitchens. But the problem was that before the food was served to the king and his subjects, it was first offered in sacrifice to the Babylonian idols.

Daniel and his friends were servants of the true God, and they didn't want to eat food that had been offered to idols. Daniel, who was the leader of these four friends, had "purposed in his heart that he would not defile himself with the portion of the king's delicacies, nor with the wine which he drank; therefore he requested of the chief of the eunuchs that he might not defile himself" (Dan. 1:8). He had made up his mind ahead of time that he would resist the temptation of the king's wonderful food, and he so informed the official who was in charge.

This chief of the eunuchs liked Daniel, but he feared the consequences if he went along with Daniel's convictions. So he said to Daniel, "I fear my lord the king, who has appointed your food and drink. For why should he see your faces looking worse than the young men who are your age? Then you would endanger my head before the king" (v. 10).

Daniel and his friends, who shared his resolve, were sympathetic to the man's fears, and so they suggested that he allow an experiment to see what would happen if they were permitted to honor God and avoid the king's food and drink. Daniel said, "Please test your servants for ten days, and let them give us vegetables to eat and water to drink. Then let our countenances be examined before you, and the countenances of the young men who eat the portion of the king's delicacies; and as you see fit, so deal with your servants" (vv. 12–13).

The official went along with their idea and "at the end of ten days their countenance appeared better and fatter in flesh than all the young men who ate the portion of the king's delicacies" (v. 15). After that, the official let them eat their own choice of food all the time.

God was pleased with the faithfulness of Daniel and his friends, and He blessed them not only physically, but also mentally.

> As for these four young men, God gave them knowledge and skill in all literature and wisdom; and Daniel had understanding in all visions and dreams. Now at the end of the days, when the king had said that they should be brought in, the chief of the eunuchs brought them in before Nebuchadnezzar. Then the king interviewed them, and among them all none was found like Daniel [and his friends]; therefore they served before the king. And in all matters of wisdom and understanding about which the king examined them, he found them ten times better than all the magicians and astrologers who were in all his realm (vv. 17–20).

God honored the holy resolve of Daniel and his friends. It should come as no surprise, then, that when Daniel's three friends were faced with great temptation later in their lives—the command that they bow and worship a statue of the king or be thrown into a fiery furnace—they again resolved to resist and were blessed by God (see Dan. 3).

Now that's a marvelous biblical story, but how do you and I purpose in our hearts to resist temptation? There are two parts to it that are summed up well in the book of James: "Therefore submit to God. Resist the devil and he will flee from you. Draw near to God and He will draw near to you" (4:7–8). We need to say no to temptation and Satan and say yes to God. Put another way, we are to turn *away* from temptation and turn *toward* God.

What this means is that you should make up your mind *now*, before you encounter temptation, that you will respond as follows when it comes along. You will not mull over whether you should indulge. You will not get just a little closer for a better look "so you can make a more intelligent decision." Instead, you will turn and run from temptation as soon as it approaches. You will run as fast and as far as the circumstances will allow. And you will call out to God in prayer, seeking His strength and wisdom through the Holy Spirit. You will allow the Scripture you've planted in your mind to come to the forefront and guide you. If necessary, you will call a Christian friend who can give you advice and encouragement.

The apostle Paul wrote, "No temptation has overtaken you except such as is common to man; but God is faithful, who will not allow you to be tempted beyond what you are able, but with the temptation will also make the way of escape, that you may be able to bear it" (1 Cor. 10:13). This great promise is quoted a lot, but it cannot be repeated too often. The person who resolves to live in holiness will face temptation having already determined to find and use the way of escape God is faithful to provide, rather than making a decision at the time of temptation whether to yield to it or not. I urge you to resolve, to purpose in your own heart, that as of right now your immediate response to all future temptations will be to turn away from them and run toward God, seeking His way out of the situation, whatever it may be.

A Call to Discipline

This entire chapter can be capsulized in the word "discipline." That's not a popular word because it conjures up images of hard work over a long period of time. Yet that is exactly what we need to live a life of holiness. Temptation comes to us time after time every day, and only discipline in the five areas we've discussed—yielding to the Holy Spirit; Bible reading, memorization, and meditation; prayer; fellowship; and purposing in our hearts to run from temptation—will let us face it victoriously. Satan and this sin-filled world will not let up in their attempts to drag us down, and so we cannot let up in our efforts to resist.

The apostle Paul was a great model of the discipline we all need, so much so that he could write to the church in Corinth, "Imitate me, just as I also imitate Christ" (1 Cor. 11:1). He said of himself: "But I discipline my body and bring it into subjection, lest, when I have preached to others, I myself should become disqualified" (1 Cor. 9:27). He also urged that we should be "bringing every thought into captivity to the obedience of Christ" (2 Cor. 10:5). As disciples of Christ, we are to live disciplined lives, for the word "disciple" and "discipline" come from the same root word. A disciple is a disciplined person.

God has called us, His servants, to a life of holiness, and He has given us the resources to live such a life. He has not left us on our own. But we must choose to use those resources and walk in them day by day. When we do, we will be servants whom God can use to reveal Himself to the world and to help change it. We will then know the peace and joy of walking in harmony with Him.

---

1. Brother Lawrence, *The Practice of the Presence of God*, trans. by E.M. Blaiklock (Nashville: Thomas Nelson, 1982), p. 20.
2. Ibid., pp. 22–23.
3. Ibid., p. 23.
4. Robert A. Cook, "Monitor Your Daydreams!" *Religious Broadcasting* (October, 1985), p. 4.
5. Ibid.
6. Ibid.
7. Ibid.

HOPE FOR THOSE
WHO FAIL

A CERTAIN MAN HAD two grown sons whom he loved very much.
One day the younger son came to him and asked for his share of
the family inheritance. This was well before the son had any right
or reason to claim his share of the family property—the division
normally would have occurred after the father died. But with a
heavy heart the father consented and gave the young man his part
of the estate.

Not long afterward, the young son gathered his things together,
converted what he owned into cash, and traveled to a faraway
country. There he spent his money recklessly and extravagantly

on riotous living—parties, prostitutes, and "good times." He indulged in every kind of wild activity about which he had ever daydreamed, never giving a second thought to his father's feelings or the values his father had taught him.

In all this time, the young man made no attempt to communicate with his family, not even to let them know where he was or that he was alive. It could well have been that the father, however, totally unknown to his wild son, kept track of where his son was and how he was doing. And every morning and evening, the father would go to the top of the hill near his house and strain his eyes in the direction toward which the son had gone, hoping fervently to catch sight of his child coming home.

The son continued his carousing, but one day he ran out of money. He didn't have anything left for food, let alone for partying. The good-time friends he had met when his money was flowing freely all disappeared. And to make matters worse, at this same time the land in which he was now living began to suffer from a severe famine. The young man found himself out on the street and very hungry and miserable.

He was desperate, and so he went to a farmer and begged for work. The man sent him into his fields to feed pigs. Now, that's an unpleasant task for most folks anyway, but this young man came from a Jewish family, and the Jews consider pigs unclean and something especially to be avoided. So this job was doubly humiliating for the young man who such a short time before had been enjoying life in the fast lane.

He was barely staying alive, and his hunger got so bad that he began to envy the pigs for the miserable food they were given. After a while in this awful state, the young man came to his senses. He realized he had sinned against God, turned his back on his father, and no longer deserved to be considered a son. But he knew, too, that even his father's servants were treated well and had more than enough to eat. So he decided to swallow his pride, return to his father, and beg for the chance to become one of his father's servants.

The next morning, he quit his job and set off for home, walking mile after dusty mile with little to eat, but with the hope that if he could make it home he would at least be able to stay alive. He probably rehearsed over and over in his mind the speech he would make to his father. As he walked day after day, he grew steadily weaker and ever more caked with dirt. His clothes were rotting into rags, and his shoes were falling apart.

Several weeks after he had started and just as his strength was about to give out, the young man entered the area where he had grown up. He knew he was now within a few miles of home, and that gave him renewed energy as he thought of the food he would find there. He also felt a new sense of dread as he anticipated the reunion with his father. His dad's love had always been clear before, but how would he react now?

The sun was beginning to set, and the young man still found himself some distance from home. What he didn't know, however, was that his father was at the top of that hill near the house, just as he had been every day since his son had left.

While the young man was yet several miles from home, his father made out the image of his son approaching. Was that his boy? He couldn't be sure at that distance, but he desperately hoped it was. He stretched up on his toes and strained his eyes to see as clearly into the distance as he could, and in a few minutes, before anyone else would have said with confidence that it was his younger son, the father was sure that that was who was coming.

Seeing the boy, the father was gripped by compassion and love for his son. He ran down the hill, calling out the boy's name all the way and moving so fast that he might have thought his lungs were going to burst if he had bothered to notice them. *But all he knew was that his son was coming home!* The servants who had been waiting with him on the hilltop could barely keep up.

When the father got to his son, he immediately threw his arms around him in a passionate hug, weeping on his neck and kissing his cheeks before the boy could say a word. The young man was overwhelmed with this reception, and the servants couldn't help but weep for joy in the obvious delight of their master.

Finally the young man gained enough composure to speak: "Father, I have sinned against heaven and in your sight, and am no longer worthy to be called your son."

Then, as the boy paused to draw a breath before asking to be considered a servant, the father turned to his servants and said, "Bring out the best robe and put it on him, and put a ring on his hand and sandals on his feet. And bring the fatted calf here and kill it, and let us eat and be merry; for this my son was dead and is alive again; he was lost and is found." And everyone in the household, when they heard the news, began to celebrate with great joy.

The Prodigal in Us All

You probably recognize this story as Jesus' parable of the Prodigal Son. It's one of the best-known stories He told (see Luke 15). The fact is there's a great deal of the Prodigal Son in all of us, and we all run from our Father occasionally. We all rebel and fail in our efforts to be holy servants; it's a part of life as sure as the sunrise. We shouldn't do it, but we do. Therefore, we need to be reminded that the forgiving Father is just as real and sure as our failure. When we fail, He stands ready to forgive us and welcome us back with open arms.

I've said repeatedly that none of us is perfect, that while we're to serve God in cleanliness of life we'll often fall short of the mark. But the point is worth emphasizing again. "All we like sheep have gone astray; we have turned, every one, to his own way" (Isa. 53:6). That's a pretty good description of all of us, isn't it, even after we become Christians. We're prone to go off in our own directions, to "do our own thing" without regard for God's will—and even in clear violation of what we know to be His will. And as the Prodigal Son found out, following one's own way may lead to temporary happiness, but true lasting joy comes only from returning to the open arms of the Father. The apostle John wrote to fellow Christians, "If we say that we have no sin, we deceive ourselves, and the truth is not in us" (1 John 1:8).

Now, of course it's not good that we fail God and sin, and when we do we usually have to suffer the consequences. But my point is that you should not be surprised and crushed when you fail. Rather, it's a fact of the human condition and you should expect it. You're no different from the rest of us, and no one is perfect. We're all prodigal sons and daughters.

The Forgiving Father

That's the first thing you need to remember from this chapter: Failure is a part of life, so don't be shocked and surprised by it. The second thing to bear in mind also comes straight from the story of the Prodigal Son: When we fail, God is patient and forgiving toward us, like the father in the parable. The father in the story loved his son and watched eagerly every day for his return. Then, when he saw his son coming, he ran to meet him, threw his arms around him and immediately restored him to his place in the family.

That picture illustrates beautifully how God relates to us when we wander off into "far countries" of sin. He waits eagerly, longingly, for us to return to His fellowship. And when we repent of our sins and turn back to Him, He is waiting for us with open arms.

Right after John said that we deceive ourselves if we say that we have no sin, he wrote, "If we confess our sins, [God] is faithful and just to forgive us our sins and to cleanse us from all unrighteousness" (1 John 1:9). James 4:8 says, "Draw near to God and He will draw near to you." I am fully convinced that if we'll take just one step in His direction after we've sinned, God will come running to greet us, just like that loving father in Jesus' story.

I emphasize this because it seems that one of the greatest problems Christians have today is our terribly inaccurate and unfair views of God and how He responds to our failures. Many believers seem to think that He's "out to get us," that He's just waiting with an avenging eye for us to fail once, and then He's going to pounce on us and make us pay dearly. Other Christians are so consumed with guilt and feelings of worthlessness, as I've discussed in previous chapters, that we think every sin is just a reaffirmation of how bad we are and that God couldn't possibly love us anymore.

If you're burdened by one of those views of God, please realize that you have misunderstood the character of God who loves you and calls you to service. You have not fully grasped the good news of the gospel. "God so loved the world" is the continual refrain all through the Bible. He loves us so much that He sent Jesus the Son to pay the price for our sins so we wouldn't have to.

Not only does God love us, but He takes the initiative in His relationship with us. Romans 5:8 tells us that "God demonstrates His own love toward us, in that *while we were still sinners*, Christ died for us" (italics mine). Revelation 13:8 describes Jesus as "the Lamb slain from the foundation of the world" for our sins. In other words, before God made the first man and woman, He knew we'd sin and *had already determined* to sacrifice His Son to pay for our rebellion. Writer Jill Briscoe describes the first sin of Eve in the Garden of Eden and says with great insight that immediately after Eve bit into the forbidden fruit, "Jesus prepared to leave for Bethlehem."[1]

The next time you fail and are tempted to doubt whether God can still love you, picture the forgiving father in the parable of the Prodigal Son as he runs to welcome his child home with open arms. That's how our heavenly Father is waiting to respond to you if you'll only turn back to Him.

In chapter 5, we saw how Israel's King David, the man after God's own heart, fell into sin with Bathsheba, first committing adultery with her and impregnating her, then ordering the murder of her husband, Uriah, and taking her for his own wife. In doing that, David showed us that even the most godly people are sometimes guilty of the deepest sins. However, in the rest of the story we also have a beautiful example of how God restores His sinful children when they turn back to Him.

The prophet Nathan, on God's orders, confronted David with his sinful crimes and told him that because of what he had done, "'Now therefore, the sword shall never depart from your house, because you have despised Me. . . . ' Thus says the Lord: 'Behold, I will raise up adversity against you from your own house. . . . ' Because by this deed you have given great occasion to the enemies of the Lord to blaspheme, the child also who is born to you shall surely die" (2 Sam. 12:10, 11, 14).

David responded by turning back to God and confessing his sin. In Psalm 51, which he wrote at that time, he said to the Lord, "Have mercy upon me, O God, according to your lovingkindness . . . blot out my transgressions. Wash me thoroughly from my iniquity, and cleanse me from my sin. For I acknowledge my transgressions, and my sin is ever before me" (vv. 1-3).

And how did God answer David's repentance? David did suffer the consequences of his sin, as God had promised: The child born to Bathsheba died shortly after birth, and David's family was forever after plagued by violence—at one point, David had to flee for his life from his own son Absalom. However, God also forgave David and restored their fellowship. Not only that, but when Bathsheba conceived again, the child who was born was Solomon, the wisest man who ever lived and the king who took Israel to its greatest glory.

Like the Prodigal Son, David turned his back on his heavenly Father and fell into great sin, the consequences of which he had to suffer. But when he turned back to his Father, He was waiting with open arms to welcome home His child. In exactly the same way, the Lord is waiting for you and me every time and however terribly we sin.

Seeing Ourselves as God Sees Us

Since God is loving and forgiving and patient toward us, we ought to be similarly gracious to ourselves. If He forgives us our sins once we confess them, we should accept His forgiveness rather than wallowing in guilt and feeling miserable and worthless. It's extremely difficult for many Christians to do, but we should forgive ourselves as God forgives us.

What we're actually doing when we refuse to forgive ourselves even after confessing our failure to God is to deny God's grace in our lives—to call Him a liar! He says our sin is forgiven, but we think and live as though it's not. Obviously, this is not right.

Perhaps it will help us to keep the proper perspective on our failures to remember that we are God's children by adoption and to think about how we relate to our own children. I knew before my first child came into the world that any kids I had would occasionally rebel against my authority and disobey me. Did that keep me from wanting a family and being thrilled when they were born? Of course not.

As my children grew, they didn't disappoint me. Sure enough, there were frequent clashes of will when they challenged the instructions of my wife and myself. Did I stop loving them, disown them, and throw them out of my house? Again, of course not. The idea is absurd. I know that children aren't perfect and that failure and rebellion are a part of the life of human beings, especially immature children. But beyond all my adult understanding of these things is the simple fact that I love my children deeply, more than my own life, and there's nothing they could ever do to make me stop loving them, no matter how much they might hurt me. (And because I love them so much, they could hurt me a very great deal if they chose to do so.) They're a part of me, and my love and concern for them will never die. I have tried to convey this love to my children so that they will *feel* that they are loved.

Our imperfect love as parents is only a poor picture of the perfect love God has for His children. He wants you to know that He loves and forgives you. His love and forgiveness can give you a freedom, a joy, and an excitement if you will accept it and begin to love and forgive yourself.

The Pain of Growing

. Did you also notice in the story of the Prodigal Son that the father allowed his younger son to go away, turn his back on the father's values, and waste his money on immoral living? He also allowed him to suffer the consequences of his decisions. The father did not force his son to stay at home, nor did he try to drag him home while he was enjoying his sinful pleasures. When the son ran out of money, he had to slop pigs to try to stay alive.

This points out that sometimes—but not always—the pain and suffering we experience are allowed by God as the practical consequences of our sin. He's not punishing us; He's just letting natural consequences of our rebellious actions take place. That approach to parenting is very different from what many of us would do today, and yet it represents the way God deals with His children.

God knows that in order for us to truly love Him, serve Him, and live in fellowship with Him, we have to do so because we want to, not because we've been forced to. Furthermore, He knows that that usually means we have to try our own way and suffer the consequences—reach the bottom of the pit, if you will—before we're willing to accept that His way is best.

Imagine what would have happened if the father of the Prodigal Son had followed his child into the far country and tried to talk him into coming home while he was still living high on the hog (pun intended!). The young man likely would have laughed in his face. As an alternative, the father could have kidnapped his son, carrying him home bound and gagged. But what would he have accomplished then? The young man's spirit would still be as rebellious as ever, and he would have run away at the first opportunity, not even bothering to ask his father's permission this time.

No, the son had to follow his chosen path to the end and see for himself how futile it was. As he sat in the muck with those pigs, he came to his senses, the Bible tells us, and realized what a mistake he had made.

In the same way, God allows us to pursue our rebellious ways until we come to our senses and see the futility of our rebellion. He knows that until we conclude for ourselves that His way really is better for us and that it's the only way to lasting joy, we will never devote ourselves wholeheartedly to Him. And that's the kind of devotion He wants.

It's a sad fact of our rebellious human nature that when things are going well for us, we tend to ignore God and go our own way. We turn to Him only when our way has led us to a point where we're suffering and in pain. Then we're only too eager to call out to Him for help! This is why C. S. Lewis in his book *The Problem of Pain* described suffering as "God's megaphone." It's only by allowing us to suffer that God can get our attention. Lewis went on to say, "God whispers to us in our pleasures, speaks in our conscience, but God shouts in our pains." Or as pastor and author

Ron Lee Davis has written, God "comes to us in our suffering not because He prefers to, but because it is often only at such times that we will accept Him."[2]

Once God has our attention and we're willing to try things His way, the struggle still isn't over. We have short memories, we're stubborn, and we fail often. We're obedient and we seek holiness for a while, but then our devotion grows cool and temptation comes and we head off on our own again. God allows us to suffer the consequences of our rebellion again, and so on it goes. As we mature spiritually, the frequency and the duration of our rebellion should decrease, but perfection awaits us only in heaven.

God's goal is to make us eventually perfectly holy, like Christ. Therefore, He wants to help us grow in every aspect of our lives. While you may turn to Him for help in one area—your temper, for instance—you will find Him speaking to you not only about your temper, but also about your pride and your materialism. C. S. Lewis described this situation using a metaphor:

> Imagine yourself as a living house. God comes in to rebuild that house. At first, perhaps, you can understand what He is doing. He is getting the drains right and stopping the leaks in the roof and so on: you knew that those jobs needed doing and so you are not surprised. But presently He starts knocking the house about in a way that hurts abominably and does not seem to make sense. What on earth is He up to? The explanation is that He is building quite a different house from the one you thought of—throwing out a new wing here, putting on an extra floor there, running up towers, making courtyards. You thought you were going to be made into a decent little cottage: but He is building a palace. He intends to come and live in it Himself.[3]

In the same book, Lewis explains the determination of God to make us fully holy one day by suggesting what Jesus would say if He were to speak to us directly:

> "Make no mistake," He says, "if you let Me, I will make you perfect. The moment you put yourself in My hands, that is what you are in for. Nothing less, or other, than that. You have free will, and if you

choose, you can push Me away. But if you do not push Me away, understand that I am going to see this job through. Whatever suffering it may cost you in your earthly life . . . whatever it costs Me, I will never rest, nor let you rest, until you are literally perfect—until My Father can say without reservation that He is well pleased with you, as He said He was well pleased with Me. This I can and will do. But I will not do anything less."[4]

If we understand that God's purpose is to make us ultimately like Christ and that our suffering as a consequence of our rebellious failures can help us find our way back to that path, then we can see that even in those situations the sovereign God is working for our good. Such an insight led Pastor Davis to write, "If the goal of our lives as Christians is to know Christ and become like Him, then ultimately we must welcome anything that will enable that process to take place."[5] That includes the suffering that results from our sins.

The suffering we experience in our lives when we fail God warns us that we have gone the wrong way and that we need to turn toward Him for forgiveness and restoration of our fellowship with Him.

Good Out of Evil

We've seen in this chapter that as much as we may desire to lead lives of holy service to God, it is inevitable that we're going to fail from time to time. But when we fail, God, our loving heavenly Father, is not only forgiving and patient, but He waits with open arms for us to come back to Him. The hardest thing for many Christians to do, however, is to accept the love and forgiveness of God. We say we know that our sins are forgiven, but we won't forgive ourselves. I urge you to accept God's forgiveness. It is then that you can know peace and joy and contentment. We've also seen that the suffering we experience when we fail God and fall into sin can actually help us grow spiritually as we recognize our need to repent and turn back to God. In that sense, our pain can be used for good.

Perhaps we can summarize this chapter by noting that we are saved by God's grace—we'll never be good enough to earn His favor—and it is God's grace that continues to lead us home. In the great love of the sovereign God we find our hope for those times when we inevitably fail in the quest for holiness. And even though we fail, we can still have lasting joy because God in His marvelous grace has forgiven us and loves us.

In the story of the Prodigal Son, in the life of David, in the lives of numerous other biblical people, as well as in the experiences of countless Christians since the close of the New Testament, this message rings through loud and clear: If you are God's child through faith in Jesus Christ, nothing you ever do can separate you from His love. However bad or guilty or unworthy you may feel, if you will turn back to Him in sincere repentance, He will come running to greet you with His arms of mercy and compassion open wide to receive you.

We call it the story of the Prodigal Son, but it's not the son who is the focus of the story. The center of the story is the father. In our churches, in our books, and in our magazines where we tell of people who—like the Prodigal Son—have wandered away from God, attention should be on Jesus Christ who forgives, not on the sinner who comes back home.

---

1. Jill Briscoe, *Prime Rib and Apple* (Grand Rapids: Zondervan, 1976), p. 19.
2. Ron Lee Davis, *Gold in the Making* (Nashville: Thomas Nelson, 1983), p. 40.
3. C. S. Lewis, *Mere Christianity* (New York: Macmillan, 1960), p. 174.
4. Ibid., p. 172.
5. Davis, p. 37.

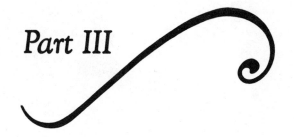

Part III

A COURAGEOUS

MESSAGE

THE CHALLENGE
TO SPEAK BOLDLY

ALTHOUGH I LOVE TO PREACH now and do it every chance I get, when God first called me, I not only didn't want to preach, but I was absolutely convinced I couldn't. You see, I had flunked tenth grade English because the teacher required every student to get up and give an oral report without any notes, and I just couldn't do it. I loved to play football before a crowd of fans. I could go out on the field and knock down the biggest guys on the other team, and that sometimes meant fellows who weighed almost three hundred pounds! Nothing made me happier than to make that other guy "eat dirt." But put me in front of a group of people and ask me to speak? No thanks!

That same timidity of speaking in front of crowds carried over into my Christian life when I was saved. Getting up in church for the first time to give my testimony about what God had done for me was a frightening and awful experience, although somehow I made it through. Then one time the young people in my church were asked to conduct an evangelistic street meeting in front of Belk's Department Store in downtown Charlotte, and they wanted me to give my testimony in public. I was very scared and very reluctant, but somehow I again made it through.

When I first sensed that God was calling me to preach, I just didn't want to do it. By that time I was willing to give my personal testimony in public, but I didn't want to make a career out of public speaking. I had had some good jobs already, and I wanted to go into business and make some money.

Still, I couldn't ignore the sense of God's calling, and so I talked to a young preacher named Jimmie Johnson. "How can a person be sure God is calling him to preach?" I asked. He told me that if God wanted me to preach, He would give me such a deep drive to do it that I wouldn't be happy doing anything else, no matter how hard I tried.

Even if I was sure God wanted me to preach, I said, I would need Bible school training, and I didn't have the money for that. Jimmie suggested we pray about it, and we did.

About a week later at a Wednesday night prayer meeting, the minister asked the young people to give a word of testimony. I gave mine, and as soon as I sat down, a well-to-do gentleman named Worth Cole got up. He looked at me and said, "If that young man who just sat down will go to college, I'll pay his first month's tuition."

Needless to say, I was shocked. But I still didn't want to preach, so I pulled out all the excuses and alibis I could think of when I talked with Jimmie Johnson again: "Jimmie, I'm kind of worried. I don't want to deny God, and yet I don't really feel that I'm supposed to be a preacher."

He looked hard at me and said, "It sounds to me as if God is trying to say He's opened the way for you but you won't walk in it."

I answered, "But I've only got the promise of one month's tuition. What will I do after that?"

He said, "What about that little word *faith*?"

Eventually I ran out of excuses and could no longer deny God's calling. I knew He wanted me to speak His message boldly as a full-time evangelist, so I went to college with only one month's tuition in my pocket. When I got there, the president of the school, being a practical man, tried to discourage me from starting the term for fear I'd just have to quit when my money ran out. He logically suggested that I go home and earn enough money to complete my training without fear of going broke and being unable to finish.

In fact, I did run out of money several times during my college career. The school would carry me for a few months, but then it would refuse to let me take exams because I was so far behind in my tuition. Every time that happened, however, God miraculously provided the money I needed, and I was able to go on. One time, for example, I was sent home, and within *one day* I got all the money I needed to bring my tuition up to date. Two days after I had left the campus, I was putting my cash on the business manager's desk. Eventually the business office stopped worrying when I fell behind on my tuition; like me, they just waited to see how God would provide next.

There was no doubt that God called me to preach His message. Likewise, there was no doubt that God called the prophet Jeremiah to proclaim boldly His courageous message. He told Jeremiah, "Whatever I command you, you shall speak. . . . Behold, I have put My words in your mouth" (Jer. 1:7, 9).

Jeremiah was a man with a clear commission from the Lord. He was called by God to be a servant. And with Jeremiah's clear call came not only God's command to live a clean life, but also a courageous message for him to proclaim. He was to speak for God, which meant he wouldn't be preaching to tickle the ears of his audience. God used Jeremiah to call the people of Judah to account for their sins and to warn of His impending judgment if they didn't repent of their evil ways and turn back to Him. This was a strong message that didn't make Jeremiah popular, but then

God is always more concerned with telling us what we need to hear rather than what we enjoy hearing.

Servanthood and God's Courageous Message

At this point, you may be thinking that there's an important difference between yourself and people like Jeremiah—namely, that his commission to boldly speak God's message was a part of his calling to "full-time Christian service" and that you're "only" a lay person. But that way of thinking misses the point.

All of us who are children of God are called to be His servants. And being a servant of God—not seeking our own will or our own advantage, but seeking to live the way Christ would want us to live—is the key to lasting joy. When God gives us His clear call, He tells us what He wants us to do and gives us the strength to do it. Some of us will be called to serve God as teachers or as construction workers or as scientists. Others will be called to serve God in "full-time Christian service." But God expects all of us who are Christians—who are called to be servants—to not only live a clean life, but to boldly proclaim a courageous message, whether we speak publicly for a living or not. There is no difference in the responsibility you and I have in this regard. God expects us to be His voice as well as His hands and His feet in this world. Jeremiah, John the Baptist, and a host of others in the Bible give us clear models of this fact.

Moreover, this world is full of sin, corruption, and injustice, whereas God is holy and just. And the more we come to know Him and become like Him, the more we also will be troubled by the sin and corruption around us and the more we will be burdened to speak God's courageous message to that world. Charles Swindoll put it this way:

> The true servant possesses an insatiable appetite for what is right, a passionate drive for justice. . . . [Being a servant means] looking around and being grieved over the corruption, the inequities, the gross lack of integrity, the moral compromises that abound. The

servant "hungers and thirsts" for right on earth. Unwilling simply to sigh and shrug off the lack of justice and purity as inevitable, the servants press on for righteousness.[1]

If our hearts beat at all in tune with that of our heavenly Father, we must speak out for God's standards when we consider the ungodly times in which we live. God is not pleased with the rampant sin in our world, and His judgment is coming against those who practice it. We are called to tell our world of His standards and warn those who knowingly violate them. This is part of the task of all of God's servants.

Now, it's fairly easy for me to say we should all speak out boldly, and quite another thing to do it, isn't it? Where does this boldness come from? After all, most of us don't have that courage naturally. We would just as soon go on our way quietly, not creating enemies for ourselves or getting anyone upset with us.

The key to this boldness lies in the fact that we don't speak for ourselves. We are identified with our Master, and we speak for Him. Thus, we know that if people reject our message, they're not rejecting us personally. Instead, they're rebelling against the God Who sent us. If we keep that perspective, we will be able to answer God's call with confidence. We can say with Jesus, "I must work the works of Him who sent Me" (John 9:4).

You may consider yourself insignificant, maybe even weak. You may think that if you tried to speak boldly about anything, no one would listen because you don't command attention.

But imagine, if you will, that you lived in a land ruled by a king who had absolute authority over his subjects. And suppose that one day he called you in to serve as his messenger to carry important orders to different parts of his domain, even though you may consider yourself to be small, weak, shy, and unimportant.

Your first thought might be that you would be totally ineffective as the king's messenger. But do you know what you'd find? Perhaps people wouldn't find you personally impressive, but they'd listen very carefully to what you had to say nonetheless, because you were speaking for the king, not yourself. As his messenger with his royal seal on the proclamation you were reading, *it would be just as if the king himself were standing in front of them*. You would be speaking with his power and his authority, not your own. In other words, the power and authority are in the message itself and the person whose message it is, not in the messenger.

You'd also find that because you were representing the king, people would respond to you in basically the same way as they'd respond to the king himself if he were standing in front of them. Of course, they'd feel a little more free to express themselves in front of you, but for the most part those who loved and respected and obeyed the king would love and respect and obey you.

On the other hand, those who did not like, respect, or obey the king would not like, respect, or obey you, either. They might even try to take out their disapproval of the king on you, verbally or otherwise. But again, this would have nothing to do with whether you were personally forceful or timid. It would be because you were representing the king to them.

Of course, the situation I've been describing isn't imaginary at all. You and I and all God's servants are called by our King to be His messengers throughout His domain. Some of us have strong personalities and handsome appearances; many of us don't. *But none of that matters*. The power and authority are in the message itself and the Person Who sent it, not in us messengers. Our job is to tell the world what the King thinks and wants, not what we think and want.

It is also true that when we speak as God's messengers, people will respond to us as they would to Him. Those who love Him will welcome and love us. On the other hand, we should expect that those who hate and oppose God will oppose us as well. Jesus said, "A servant is not greater than his master. If they persecuted Me, they will also persecute you. If they kept My word, they will keep yours also. But all these things they will do to you for My name's sake, because they do not know Him who sent Me" (John 15:20–21).

Bold Speaking and Responsibility

Since we are to proclaim God's message, not our own, He is ultimately responsible for the outcome, not us. The results are in the hands of the Master, not the servant. In other words, it's not our job to change the hearts of men or the course of history— only God can do those things. Thus, He will not judge us by whether we've done what only He can do. Instead, He'll judge us according to whether we've done what He has asked us to do, which is to proclaim His courageous message. But the impact that message has is up to Him.

Let me give you a concrete example of what I mean. Billy Graham has been given a specific calling from God to be an evangelist, to tell people of their sinfulness and the redeeming love of God, to call them to repentance and reconciliation with the Lord who gave His Son to save them. *But Billy is not accountable for the response of a single individual to that message.* It is up to the individuals themselves, as God speaks to their hearts, to make a choice either for or against God.

Billy Graham can't save anyone, and he can't make decisions for people. If he is faithful in proclaiming God's message clearly and accurately, he has done what God wants of him. The results are in God's hands.

What this means is that we don't need to be burdened with a sense of personal responsibility for the apparent effectiveness or ineffectiveness of the message God gives us to deliver. Our job is just to deliver it; God's job is to use it as He sees fit.

Of course it's frustrating and discouraging if no one seems to be responding when you speak for God, and of course you should care about the people you're trying to reach. Billy Graham and the rest of us on his team would be overjoyed if everyone wanted to come forward at every crusade meeting we held. But we know that's not going to happen. Hundreds and even thousands respond each night, but a larger number stay in their seats.

Why do some come forward and others don't, when they all heard the same message?

There are many factors at work, of course, including the simple truth that many of the people in the audience are already saved. But the most basic fact is that while we trust God is speaking to every heart, individuals are making their own choices about how they'll respond to Him. Many are ready to commit themselves to the Lord at a particular meeting and so go forward, but many others are not. Perhaps among the latter are some whom God has called but who are not yet ready to yield to His lordship. And maybe Billy's role in their lives is to plant a seed that will someday yield fruit for another of God's servants to harvest.

What would happen to Billy, however, if he did not leave the outcome of his crusades in the hands of the sovereign God? Instead of being able to rejoice in the salvation of those who come forward, he would be crushed by despair over the majority of people who stay in their seats. He would see himself as a failure rather than as a servant who had faithfully executed the task he had been given as God's messenger.

There's another important lesson for us in the truth that God is responsible for the outcome of the message He gives us to deliver. Speaking God's message boldly will sometimes get us into embarrassing situations or the kind of opposition Jesus talked about in John 15. It's not an easy thing to stand up for God in a world that has largely rejected Him. And at such times, it's a tremendous comfort to know that the outcome is in His hands, and that He is looking with favor on His faithful servants. This, too, can give us the strength to go forward.

Hebrews 11 is known as the "faith chapter" of the Bible. In it are the stories of many of God's servants who endured great ridicule and opposition to do and say the things God wanted them to do and say because they had faith in Him—because they left the outcome of their obedience in His hands. We could look at any of these to find great inspiration for our lives today, and I would encourage you to read that chapter over and over. But let's look briefly at just one of these people.

No doubt you remember the story of Noah and the ark, which is recorded in Genesis 6-9. In the time of Noah, thousands of years ago, all of humanity except Noah and his family had rejected God and chosen to live in continual sinfulness. God was even sorry that He had made people. In His righteous judgment, God destroyed all the human and animal life on earth through a global flood brought on by forty straight days and nights of torrential rain.

Before the rains came, however, God instructed Noah to build a boat that would house him and his family and a small number of every species of animal, protecting them from the flood. These people and animals would repopulate the earth after the floodwaters subsided.

Noah was obedient to God's command and set about building the ark as God had instructed. Now, this was a big boat, and it undoubtedly took Noah some time to finish it. His neighbors had a long time to ridicule him and make his life miserable. They didn't obey God, and so they would have refused to believe Noah when he warned them that God was going to judge the world with a global flood.

Try to imagine what Noah's life must have been like for those years. No one believed him and no one supported him outside his family—and they probably had their doubts, too! People came by to watch him work and throw taunts and insults at him: "How's your boat coming along, Noah? Isn't the sky bright and clear today? You don't really think God—if He exists at all—is going to flood the whole world, do you? Why don't you quit before everyone concludes you've gone crazy?" No doubt some of Noah's "friends" tried that last line on him.

Life must have been extremely difficult indeed for Noah while he was building the ark. But the key to his perseverance was that he trusted God and did what he was told, leaving the responsibility for the results where it belonged—with the Lord. Hebrews 11 says of Noah, "By faith Noah, being divinely warned of things not yet seen, moved with godly fear, prepared an ark for the saving of his household, by which he condemned the world and became heir of the righteousness which is according to faith" (v. 7).

Manford Gutzke summarized this truth well when he said, "A servant may know that the particular conduct he is following [or message he is proclaiming] will lead him into embarrassing situations, and may actually expose him to being mistreated. He may know that this conduct will be misunderstood. . . . But if it is the thing that he should do, he will go ahead and do [or say] it, regardless. The servant leaves the ultimate outcome in the Master's hands."[2]

Bold Speaking and Freedom

It's not pleasant to consider the opposition or embarrassment that may come our way when we obey God and speak His message boldly, even when we're willing to leave the results in His hands and we bolster our faith by remembering the examples of people like Noah. But there is a positive side to proclaiming God's message courageously and that's the tremendous sense of freedom we can experience as we walk in obedience. Let's look at the nature of this freedom.

All of us are driven, to one extent or another, by pride. Generally, we're more driven by pride than we would like to admit even to ourselves. We want to be—and want others to consider us to be—the best, the smartest, the most attractive, the most fun, and yes, the most spiritual, too. Because this is so, we're constantly evaluating people, words, and events from a self-centered and self-serving perspective. We're always comparing ourselves, our achievements, and our possessions against those of others. We seek to live up to the expectations of those who are important to us so they'll think the best of us.

If we seek to serve God in word and action and leave the results to Him, however, we can enjoy a tremendous freedom that breaks the chains of pride and delivers us from that endless losing game of self-centered comparisons. Charles Swindoll wrote about this experience in his life:

My fierce tendency to compete with others started to diminish. My insecure need to win—*always* win—also started to fade. Less and less was I interested in comparing myself with other speakers and pastors. This growing, healthy independence freed me to be *me*, not a mixture of what I thought others expected me to be. And now my heart really goes out to others when I see in them that misery-making "comparison syndrome" that held me in its grip for so many years.[3]

Richard Foster wrote of this freedom in these terms: "In the discipline of service there is also great liberty. Service enables us to say 'no!' to the world's games of promotion and authority. It abolishes our need (and desire) for a 'pecking order.'"[4]

Yes, in giving ourselves and our service to God, we enjoy a wonderful freedom. This is something that doesn't happen easily or overnight. Remember C. S. Lewis's image of the castle God is slowly, steadily making out of each of us. We grow in this as in all other aspects of holiness. But the freedom is there for us to gain as we continue to walk with Him. And freedom brings lasting joy.

Speaking Boldly in Love

God is responsible for the results of our bold speaking, and that can give us a great freedom. But we must be careful to understand that we do not have the freedom to be irresponsible. There are two thoughts that need to temper our bold proclamations of God's courageous message.

First, we need to remember that because we're speaking for God and not for ourselves, we need to take care that we're truly representing Him. In other words, we must be able to say honestly that the courageous message we are proclaiming is His and not ours. We must be sure we are not abusing "thus saith the Lord" to grind our own axes or pursue our own ends.

It is bad enough to lie when we're speaking only for ourselves. To lie in God's name, to mislead people about God and His purposes, is infinitely worse. Nor do we want to speak falsely out of ignorance. Before we presume to speak for God, we must be very sure that we have discerned His will and His message correctly so that we can present it accurately.

To have this kind of confidence when we speak, we need to be people of prayer, people of humility, and people who study and know God's Word so we can interpret it accurately to our needy world. A royal messenger has to get the King's message right or he isn't much of a messenger. And for Christian servants, that means knowing our King and the things about Him that He has already revealed to us in the Bible.

The second concern that tempers our freedom to proclaim a courageous message is that anything we do or say must be motivated and shaped and characterized by love. Love is the hallmark of the Christian, and we do not throw it out the window when we stand to speak for God. We must speak against injustice because we know it grieves our Father, for example, but we must love both the victims and the perpetrators of the injustice.

Of course, speaking in love does not mean we never say things that would upset or displease other people. Sometimes love forces us to say things that cause others distress. If I see a young child reaching for a hot stove, for example, love prompts me to try to stop the child from touching it, even if he really wants to put his hand on it, and even if my shouting at him hurts his feelings. Likewise, if I see sinful activity in the world around me, love compels me to warn those involved that they must repent of it and turn to God or else face His judgment.

The motivation of love also affects how we respond to our critics and opponents. In fact, the way we treat our critics and opponents says a lot more about what kind of servants of God we are than the way we treat our friends. Jesus didn't condemn even the people who unjustly crucified Him, but instead He prayed for them, asking the heavenly Father to forgive them.

Billy Graham is a great example to me in this area. He has had many critics through the years, but I have never seen him argue with them or respond to them out of bitterness. Instead, his answers are factual, sometimes humorous, and always marked by humility. Indeed, he has asked those of us on his team to pray that the things our critics say about us would never become true. I see in his responses a nature that has been shaped by a long and close walk with God.

I find it difficult sometimes to respond to critics out of love. I have a temper, and some of the people I have encountered in my years with Billy have done or said things that have made me want to respond in a distinctly unloving way. But because I know I represent him and the rest of the team, I have managed with God's help to control my tongue on a number of occasions when I was sorely tempted to say something that was not motivated by love and that I would have regretted later. I thank God for helping me.

Loving our opponents also means forgiving and forgetting the offenses they commit against us. We must not allow the past to have a negative influence on the present or the future. Otherwise, every time we deal with our opponents the relationship will be clouded by those past differences, and we won't be able to love them and treat them as we should.

Perhaps a word picture will help you understand what it means to forgive *and* forget. Someone has said that when God forgives our sins, He buries them in the deepest part of the ocean, and that's what it means for us to forgive too. When we refuse to forget as well as forgive, however, it's as if we get in a boat with our fishing gear every once in a while and paddle our way out there to bring up the offense again. But God puts up a sign that says *"No Fishing,"* and that's what it means to forget. We don't go fishing for the offense any more. We let it stay buried for good.

Says Charles Swindoll, refusing to forget "means we have erected a monument of spite in our mind, and that isn't really forgiveness at all. Servants must be big people. Big enough to *go on*, remembering the right and forgetting the wrong."[5]

Guidelines for Bold Speaking

In the next chapter we'll look at some of the issues of our day that I believe are a part of the courageous message God wants His servants to proclaim. But first, we need some guidelines for determining when and how we should speak boldly and how we can do so with confidence.

First, as I said earlier, we need to be careful that anything we would say on behalf of God accurately reflects His will. This requires us to be people of prayer, people of the Word, and people with a deep humility. It also means we have to scrutinize our words for any hint of pride, self-promotion, or self-seeking.

Second, we must be sure that what we say is consistent with the Word of God. For one thing, this means that in speaking for God we truly speak out of His Word and not out of what our culture finds acceptable or unacceptable. I spoke earlier about the dangers of legalism, and many who are legalists proclaim their beliefs as if they were the Word of God when they are not.

You will find nothing in the Bible, for instance, that condemns long hair on men, yet many ministers have preached against it. It may be inadvisable for most men in our society for other reasons, but to claim to speak for God and declare long hair on men to be sinful is just plain wrong.

Matters such as length of hair are clearly issues that grow out of concerns with our current culture. There may be good reason for those concerns, and biblical teaching does have relevance to them, but one must be very careful when one wants to say that "this view and this view alone represents the will of God in this matter."

Moreover, when we speak for God, we must test what we say by His Word to make sure it is in no way contrary to that Word. God will never ask us to do or say anything that doesn't agree with His will as He has already revealed it to us in the Bible.

The issue comes up frequently when people speak what is said to be "a word from God" or "a word of prophecy." Whenever a message is thought to come from God, it should be tested against the teaching of the Bible. We know for certain that the Bible came from the Lord, and He would never contradict Himself.

Third, any message from God will glorify Christ. The Bible tells us that God intends "that at the name of Jesus every knee should bow, of those in heaven, and of those on earth, and of those under the earth, and that every tongue should confess that Jesus Christ is Lord, to the glory of God the Father" (Phil. 2:10–11). Since this is God's desire, any message from Him will serve that purpose.

Fourth, a message from God will build up rather than tear down the church, which is Christ's body on earth. God gives spiritual gifts for the building up, or edification, of the church, and it is always His will that the church prosper spiritually and be characterized by love among its members for one another. There will be disagreements among Christians, of course, which is why we have various denominations. And sin in the church must be dealt with, which is why church discipline is essential. But even when we disagree and when individuals have to be disciplined, the *motive* should be the strengthening of the church and the loving correction of the individual.

Finally, it should be obvious, but it is worth stating clearly, that any message from God will be true in every respect. God is a God of truth and of holiness. There is no darkness and no falsehood in Him. Therefore, we must take care when we presume to speak for Him that not the slightest lie is to be found in what we say.

One of the lies that is probably almost as old as humanity itself is the notion that the end justifies the means, that as long as you are pursuing a good goal, you are justified in doing whatever it takes—however bad—to reach that goal. Unfortunately, some who sincerely seek to serve God have bought that lie, and the result is that half-truths and outright deception are sometimes used when such people speak on behalf of God. These are false messengers who damage their own credibility and God's in the eyes of the world.

It is an awesome thing to speak for God, and reading this chapter may have made you afraid to try lest you somehow misrepresent Him. But He expects His servants to proclaim a courageous message on His behalf. If you are hesitant to speak God's message, you need to remember that there is much that God would have us speak to the world that is already very plain for us to see in His Word. Moreover, other mature Christians can help you evaluate the correctness of what you believe is God's message for you to proclaim.

Also, it is usually better to be bold and risk making a mistake—as long as your motives are right—than to sit back and say nothing. I have said repeatedly that we're all going to fail from time to time as we seek to serve God, so don't hold back waiting for the day when you think you can represent God perfectly. They'll put you in your grave before that day comes!

God will make it clear how and when He wants you to proclaim a courageous message. Let me begin your thinking by pointing out in the next chapter some of those issues about which I believe God wants His servants to be speaking boldly today.

---

1. Charles R. Swindoll, *Improving Your Serve*, pp. 106–7.
2. Manford George Gutzke, *Born to Serve*, p. 76.
3. Swindoll, pp. 93–94.
4. Richard Foster, *Celebration of Discipline*, pp. 110–11.
5. Swindoll, p. 70.

9

THE ISSUES
OF OUR DAY

IMAGINE THAT A YOUNG BOY has caught a frog and that, as boys are apt to do, he wants to experiment with it a little. Suppose that since frogs live in water most of the time, the boy wants to see how his frog will react if the water it's in gets hot.

The boy might start his test by heating a pot of water to boiling. If he then tries to drop the frog into the pot, his experiment will be over in a hurry. You see, the frog may not be smart, but it's not stupid, either. If you throw it into a pot of boiling water, it's going to feel right away that the water is too hot, and it will jump out of there as soon as it hits the water.

But suppose the boy heats the pot of water just until it's comfortably warm, and then he puts in his frog. The frog will splash around a little, enjoying it. If the boy continues to turn up the heat gradually, the frog won't even notice it's getting hotter and hotter. His body will adjust to each slight change in temperature until it can't adjust any more. If this goes on long enough, the boy will have a cooked frog on his hands.

Something very much like this frog-cooking process has been happening to the church of Jesus Christ. The culture in which we live has us in a pot of water, and it has been slowly turning up the temperature over a period of years. The result is that we're getting seriously cooked, and often we're not even aware of it.

This is not a phenomenon unique to our day, of course. Satan has always tried to seduce God's people and undermine their influence in the world. That's why in every generation God has called His servants to speak boldly, to proclaim a courageous message. But it does seem to me that we're not as aware of our predicament as Christians have been in generations past. And the deterioration that we see both around us and in the church itself today leads us to consider the issues of our time about which God is calling His servants to speak out boldly on His behalf.

What are the issues about which we should be concerned? I want to address six of them in this chapter, but before I do, a few words of explanation are in order.

First, as I said in the last chapter, it's an awesome thing to speak for God, and it's easy to be presumptuous and speak out of one's own opinions and biases rather than really representing Him. Nonetheless, we must not allow that realization to keep us silent. God has commanded us to proclaim a courageous message, and we must do so.

Second, just as God calls His children to be involved in different tasks, so He also calls us to speak to different issues as He lays unique burdens on each one of our hearts. In other words, while the six issues I'm going to address here are all important, the Lord may be asking you to speak to other concerns. And that's okay. But you certainly need to be aware of these issues because they are six of the most important ones today.

Third, not only may God be calling you to speak out on issues other than the six I'm going to discuss, but you may even disagree with some of what I say about them. While I obviously believe I'm right and will try to support what I say biblically, I also recognize that few individuals—including Christians—agree on every issue.

Not only *won't* we agree on every issue, but we *shouldn't*. As the late journalist Walter Lippmann said with great wisdom, "When all think alike, no one thinks very much." God speaks to each of us and reveals Himself to us as individuals, and much that is in His Word is subject to varying interpretations by sincere believers in Jesus Christ. So even if you find yourself disagreeing with some of what I say on one or more of the issues I'm about to address, at least acknowledge that they are the honest efforts of a sincere fellow-Christian to discern God's will in these areas, and give them careful and prayerful consideration.

With those understandings as background, let's look at some issues that I believe God would have His servants speak to today. The first two are really as old as the church, and they're foundational to the Christian faith and life. Because they are so important, they are still being challenged after all these years as Satan attempts to weaken the faith of God's people.

The Deity of Jesus Christ

The first issue—the deity of Jesus Christ—is absolutely vital to the Christian faith. In fact, if you do not believe in the deity of Jesus Christ, I do not believe you can honestly claim to be a Christian. The deity of Jesus Christ means that in addition to being fully human like you and me, He was also fully God and sinlessly perfect.

You don't find many people today who try to argue that Jesus never lived, that He was just a figment of Christians' imaginations. Likewise, few would suggest today that He was not a human being with a body just like ours, that He only had the appearance of a normal body but was really very different from us. In the early years of the church, there was a popular heresy called gnosticism that argued just that, but it's not heard much today.

What you do hear, however, is people telling us that Jesus wasn't fully God. They say that He was a good man, maybe even the best who ever lived. But while they will grant that much, they will draw the line at the assertion that He was fully God as well as man.

An understanding and belief in the deity of Christ is important because it is precisely at this point that many cults and other religions reveal that they are not teaching the truth. Jehovah's Witnesses, for instance, say that Jesus is not God, but that He is one of many gods. Muslims revere Jesus as a great prophet and godly person, but there is little difference, they say, between Him and Abraham, Moses, or Mohammed; Jesus is not God. While we might expect such teaching from a member of a cult or another religion, we need to be aware that even some who call themselves Christians will question the deity of Jesus Christ. They have a right to do that, of course, but they should not call themselves Christians. That's heresy!

There are two vital reasons why a Christian must accept and believe in the deity of Jesus Christ. The first is that it is the clear testimony of the Bible, especially of Jesus Himself. Thus, if we deny His deity, we're calling Him a liar or else claiming He's a madman. Those are our choices. It's that simple. And second, His deity is essential to our salvation. If Jesus isn't God, we're still guilty of our sins and without hope. The apostle Paul pointed this out when talking about Christ's resurrection: "If Christ is not risen, your faith is futile; you are still in your sins" (1 Cor. 15:17).

We can find evidence for Jesus' deity in many places. We can look at the witness of His perfect life, the miracles He performed, or the fact of His bodily resurrection three days after His crucifixion. We can look at parts of Scripture outside the Gospels that verify His deity such as when Paul wrote to Titus that we should be "looking for the blessed hope and glorious appearing of our great God and Savior Jesus Christ" (Titus 2:13).

We also have the inspired witness of the apostle John, who told us, "In the beginning was the Word [Jesus], and the Word was with God, and the Word was God. He was in the beginning with God. All things were made through Him, and without Him nothing was made that was made. . . . And the Word became flesh and dwelt among us, and we beheld His glory, the glory as of the only begotten of the Father, full of grace and truth" (John 1:1–3, 14).

The best place to look, however, is at the words of Jesus Himself. He made His deity plain on numerous occasions. Once, for example, when He was talking to His adversaries, they mentioned Abraham, who had lived several thousand years earlier. We pick up the story with Jesus speaking:

> "Most assuredly, I say to you, if anyone keeps My word he shall never see death." Then the Jews said to Him, "Now we know that You have a demon! Abraham is dead, and the prophets; and You say, 'If anyone keeps My word he shall never taste death.' Are You greater than our father Abraham, who is dead? And the prophets are dead. Whom do You make Yourself out to be?" Jesus answered, "If I honor Myself, My honor is nothing. It is My Father who honors Me, of whom you say that He is your God. Yet you have not known Him, but I know Him. And if I say, 'I do not know Him,' I shall be a liar like you; but I do know Him and keep His word. Your father Abraham rejoiced to see My day, and he saw it and was glad." Then the Jews said to Him, "You are not yet fifty years old, and have You seen Abraham?" Jesus said to them, "Most assuredly, I say to you, before Abraham was, I AM." Then they took up stones to throw at Him (John 8:51–59).

Why did His opponents want to stone Him? Because they understood very well that Jesus was claiming to be God by saying that even before Abraham's day, thousands of years before, He had been alive. That would be true of no one but God. Not only that, but in describing Himself as "I AM," Jesus was using the name by which God had identified Himself to Moses in the burning bush in Exodus 3. There was no doubt in the minds of these people about what Jesus was claiming concerning Himself.

I would encourage you to read also passages like John 5:16–23 and 10:22–33, where Jesus again clearly asserted His deity and His opponents had no doubt what He was claiming. What we must conclude from such passages was summed up extremely well by C. S. Lewis:

> I am trying here to prevent anyone saying the really foolish thing that people often say about Him: "I'm ready to accept Jesus as a great moral teacher, but I don't accept His claim to be God." That is the one thing we must not say. A man who was merely a man and said the sort of things Jesus said would not be a great moral teacher. He would either be a lunatic—on the level with the man who says he is a poached egg—or else he would be the Devil of Hell. You must make your choice. Either this man was, and is, the Son of God; or else a madman or something worse. You can shut Him up for a fool, you can spit at Him and kill Him as a demon; or you can fall at His feet and call Him Lord and God. But let us not come with any patronizing nonsense about His being a great human teacher. He has not left that open to us. He did not intend to.[1]

Thus, our choice is to believe Jesus or not, but let there be no mistake about what He claimed. Because of the testimony of God's Word, because of all that Jesus said and did, because of the testimony of the church down through the centuries, and because of the witness of the Holy Spirit in my heart, I believe by faith that Jesus Christ is indeed God, the second member of the Trinity, and that this is the stand that God's people must always take without compromise. As Jesus Himself said, "He who does not honor the Son does not honor the Father who sent Him" (John 5:23).

Why is Jesus' deity essential to our salvation? The reason the human race needed saving is that while God is holy, totally pure and without sin as the Bible declares repeatedly (see Isa. 6:3), we are sinful and fall far short of His glory (see Rom. 3:23). Because God is also just (see Ps. 89:14), He must judge sin, and He could not allow those who were guilty to spend eternity in heaven with Himself. Since even the smallest sin disqualified us and we are all full of sin, we were all without hope of ever being reconciled to God. God also said that forgiveness for our sins and reconciliation with Himself comes only through the death and shedding of blood of a sinless substitute (see Heb. 9:22).

The help we needed could come only from God. Our sole hope was for someone to live a perfect life on this earth, sinless like God, and then be willing to pay the death penalty the rest of us deserved for our sins. But since all men and women are born with a sin nature and then sin by choice throughout their lives, where was such a person to be found? Jesus Christ, God the Son Himself, became man, lived that life of perfection, and then voluntarily died in our place, taking upon Himself the punishment for sin that we deserved. As Paul wrote in 2 Corinthians 5:21, "He [God the Father] made Him who knew no sin [Jesus] to be sin for us, that we might become the righteousness of God in Him."

Do you see why Jesus' deity is so important? If He weren't God as well as man, He couldn't have lived a sinless life. And if His life weren't sinless, He could have died only for His own sins, not for ours. We would have been doomed to eternal separation from God as the penalty for our sins. As we saw in chapter 2, however, because Jesus offered His sinless life in our place, we have the opportunity to become children of God by faith (see John 1:12).

Because the deity of Christ is vital to God's plan of salvation— and this is one issue on which I do *not* think true Christians can disagree—this doctrine provides a good test of any group that claims to be Christian. If you're concerned about any church, any new religious group, or any group that you've heard identified as a cult, look into what it says about Jesus. If the members refuse to say that He is the only begotten Son of God, very God Himself—if they claim He is only a good man, a great teacher, a prophet, one of many messengers from God—you'll know they are not Christian. They may sound Christian by using Christian terminology, and they may insist they are true believers, but if they try to make Jesus less than He is, they are deceiving you.

Jesus is the cornerstone of our faith. His deity is essential to our salvation, as well as to the reliability of the Bible, for it clearly and repeatedly asserts His deity. If the Bible is wrong about that, we can't trust what it says about anything else, either. By the same token, those who deny the deity of Christ make God Himself out to be a liar. As servants of God, therefore, we must boldly proclaim the deity of Jesus Christ in the face of all who try to convince the world of any lie to the contrary.

The Inspiration of Scripture

A second foundational issue, one that is much in dispute today, is the inspiration of Scripture. It is so important because the trustworthiness of the Bible is crucial to the Christian faith and life. In the Bible we learn truths about God and ourselves. We learn of His love and His plan for humanity. And we learn how He wants us to live and of the resources He gives us for that life.

At the risk of oversimplifying the current debate about the Bible, the basic question is whether the Bible is the inspired Word of God—true in every detail and authoritative for doctrine and practice, just as relevant and binding on the church today as when it was written—or whether it contains mistakes because it was written by flawed men, men who were sometimes writing about subjects, like science, that they didn't really understand, and men who were sometimes addressing issues in a way that was colored by the culture and customs of their day and so no longer applies in our age.

I believe in the verbal, plenary inspiration of the Scriptures in the original autographs. Let me explain briefly what that means. The Bible was written by many different people over a period of several thousand years. The last book to be written was completed nineteen hundred years ago. Furthermore, different parts of it were written in different languages—Hebrew, Greek, and Aramaic. But when the writers first wrote those original books of our Bible (the original autographs), they wrote all of what is now the Scriptures—every book, chapter, and paragraph—under the direct guidance of the Holy Spirit (plenary inspiration). He used their personalities and their vocabularies, but He superintended the choice of every word (verbal inspiration) so that the message recorded was exactly what God wanted to say. The Bible is not just a useful body of human ideas. It makes clear the mind of God Himself.

Now, as far as we know, none of those original Bible manuscripts has survived to this day. Instead, men of God down through the centuries have continually made copies of the Scriptures as older copies wore out, so that even the oldest manuscripts we have today are many copies removed from the originals.

When documents are copied by hand so many times, it is to be expected that a few small mistakes might creep in. However, the Holy Spirit has guided this work as well, and our Bibles today are very close to those original autographs—certainly on all matters vital to our faith. When we compare biblical manuscripts made at different periods of history, we find the accuracy and consistency of the work to be magnificent. God has truly preserved His Word for us!

Still, there have been some small typographical errors made in the copying process over the centuries, so we can't claim that the Bibles we have today are *absolutely* without error the way the original manuscripts were. The mistakes that have been found are insignificant, however, and the important matters of our faith are accurately preserved in our modern Bibles. This is beyond dispute.

I believe in the inspiration of the Bible as I've explained it because the Bible itself makes this claim on its own behalf. Perhaps the best-known verse to do this is 2 Timothy 3:16: "All Scripture is given by inspiration of God, and is profitable for doctrine, for reproof, for correction, for instruction in righteousness." That word "inspiration" literally means that Scripture, which is inspired of God, is "God-breathed." The picture we're given is of God Himself speaking His Word, which the biblical authors recorded for us under the guidance of the Holy Spirit.

We also read in 2 Peter 1:20–21: "Knowing this first, that no prophecy of Scripture is of any private interpretation [or origin], for prophecy never came by the will of man, but holy men of God spoke as they were moved by the Holy Spirit." Here again is a strong assertion that the Bible is God's own Word, not the invention of any person.

Space prevents me from even listing the hundreds of prophecies in the Bible that have already come true and that further validate its claim to be the Word of God. It also prevents me from citing the many occasions when Jesus quoted from various parts of the Old Testament in such a way as to indicate that He clearly considered all Scripture to be the true, authoritative message of God.

These are some of the reasons why I believe the Bible to be the inspired Word of God. But why is this issue so important now? The reason is that many people, including numerous Christians, have adopted a lesser view of Scripture in the last few decades, and I fear the church of Christ has suffered as a result.

There is nothing wrong with critically evaluating the text of Scripture in an effort to determine scribal errors so that we will have a text more nearly like the original autographs. Tremendous work has been done in this regard during this century. And there is nothing wrong with studying the culture of Bible times in an effort to better understand the meaning of what the biblical writers said. Understanding the hatred between the Jews and the Samaritans, for instance, helps us to better understand the parable of the Good Samaritan. But when someone sets up his opinions as being of more importance than the statements of Scripture, that is wrong. Then we are no longer under the authority of the Word of God, but under the authority of the particular person who is interpreting the Bible. For example, the Bible assumes that there is a God and that God can use His servants to prophesy the future. Some scholars, however, do not believe such prophecy can occur. When they approach the book of Daniel, therefore, with its remarkable prophecies that were fulfilled by the time of Christ, such scholars have to assume that the book was not written by the man who it says wrote it—Daniel—but by someone who lived after the fulfillment of the prophecies came about. Thus, the Bible is not the judge of the opinions of these scholars, but their opinions are the judge of the Bible. Given the choice, I will take the authority of the Bible any day.

The first problem with a lesser view of Scripture is that once you decide the entire Bible isn't inspired and certain parts are wrong or are based on customs that no longer apply, who's to say the entire book isn't full of error—including the parts that spell out God's plan of salvation? When the Bible claims to be God's authoritative Word and you assert that it is in error in just one significant place, you have cast the validity of the entire book into question, and that could be disastrous to anyone's faith.

A second problem growing out of the first is that if the Bible is judged to be unreliable in presenting God's message to humanity, we are left without a trustworthy guidebook for life. There is no one sure standard to which we can all look; we're left in a confusion of individual interpretations of which parts of Scripture are true and authoritative. Surely this is not what God wants.

A third problem is that, as with the deity of Jesus Christ, when people deny the claims God has made that the Bible was given by His inspiration, they are calling Him a liar. I assure you He does not take kindly to that.

I know that biblical scholars who disagree with my stand on inspiration will accuse me of grossly over-simplifying the issue. But I think it really boils down to the simple question of whether you believe what the Bible says about itself in such clear passages as 2 Timothy 3:16.

Because it goes right to the heart of the authority for our faith, the inspiration of the Bible is one of the issues of our day about which I believe God wants His servants to be speaking boldly.

The Influence of Television

The deity of Christ and the inspiration of Scriptures are two issues that have been with the church from its beginning, and they are no less important today than they ever were because they are central to our faith. But I now want us to consider some issues that, while they are not foundational to Christianity, are still very important as we seek God's will for our culture. Most of these are relatively recent concerns. The first is the influence of television on our society and in our individual lives.

Television, of course, is a brand-new phenomenon in historical terms. It has been with us for less than forty years. That's hard to imagine because there's now at least one television set in almost every American home, and we spend huge amounts of time in front of it. The typical child growing up today spends far more time watching TV than he does in school, and adults also spend many hours with it. Is it any wonder, then, that this medium exerts a tremendous influence on the thinking and values of our society?

When television first became available to the public, many Christians considered it a bad thing and refused even to buy sets. Clearly, however, most Christians no longer think that way. Perhaps that attitude was an overreaction, and television *is* capable of doing much good, but we need to look carefully at what this devotion to "the tube" has done to us.

I have two major concerns related to television—two issues about which God wants His servants to proclaim a courageous message. The first has to do with how much time we spend with television and how that time is spent. When the typical family puts in its hours in front of the TV each day, the members of that family might as well be in separate houses because television viewing for the most part is a solitary experience. Two people may be in the same room watching the same program, but they rarely speak to each other, except perhaps during commercials. Instead, each is lost in his own thoughts, his own little world, his own reactions to the program.

Families today are very busy, as we've discussed already. What's needed is not less interaction, but more. When the kids come home from school and Dad (and maybe Mom, too) gets home from work, it's so easy to switch on the set and plop down in front of it for the night. The kids may even go into a different room to watch the second TV if they don't like what the folks are watching. But we need to be talking to each other about what happened during the day and what's important to us, playing games together, working together, and encouraging one another. And those things just don't happen when our attention is riveted to the TV.

I saw a documentary the other night on television about a family that lived before the age of TV. The narrator talked about how active the family always stayed doing things together and how it was unusual for them to sit still for long, even to get a family portrait taken. I remember thinking, *Boy, those people were lucky not to have television. What a great time they had together. If they had had a TV, they probably would have done a lot less.*

I really think that by and large, families were better off before television came along, simply because they had more time to talk together, read together, sing together, play together, go on hikes together, have devotions together, and do all the other things that build up a family. Billy Graham and other Christian broadcasters have been allowed by God to make tremendous use of television, but all things considered, I still believe that the average family would be much better off if it gave a lot less of its time—or even no time at all—to television.

My first concern about television is the amount of time we give to it. My second concern is with the content of what we see and the influence television has on us. Our minds are wonderful computers, and they never forget a single thing that's fed into them. We certainly don't remember everything we've seen and heard on a conscious level; the mind filters out what it considers unimportant. But even what's filtered out gets stored away and works on the subconscious mind, helping to form our perception of the world and our values. This is why it's so important that we be careful about what we watch, read, and listen to, even when we're relaxing—maybe especially then, because then we're not actively questioning what we see. And that's why we need to be concerned about the influence of anything that we allow to feed our minds as much as we do television.

It's no surprise for me to say that the message of commercial television is not at all Christian. It tells us that what's important in life is the pursuit of wealth and power, that sexual immorality is great "as long as no one is hurt," and that enjoying this life is all that matters because there's certainly nothing else.

Television has played a large role in the "slow boiling" of the church to which I referred at the beginning of the chapter, especially in the areas of language and sexual mores. As the values of the society have changed gradually, TV has reflected those shifting standards, and we've kept right on watching.

Years ago, a friend of mine was in a terrible car crash. Because of the head injuries he suffered, he forgot the preceding seven years of his life. It was especially tragic because he had been married and had a child during that time, and he didn't remember any of it. One night as he and his family were watching television together after the accident, a program came on that included some things that seemed inoffensive to the rest of the group. But to this Christian who was now living seven years in the past, so to speak, the program was shocking. "How can you look at things like this?" he asked. When his family looked critically at the program, they decided he was right and turned it off.

Most of us, however, haven't had seven years wiped from our memories, and things that might have shocked us with good reason seven years ago are things that we now let television feed into us every day. That's because the changes have come gradually, and like the frog, we've adjusted slowly as the water heated up, never noticing that we were being boiled.

I'm also bothered by the programmers' attitude toward God and Christianity. For the most part, the image we get is that normal people never go to church, never pray, never take religious values into account when making decisions, and never even think about God. This is amazing when you stop to realize that a recent Gallup survey showed that 79 percent of the American public claim to have made a personal commitment to Jesus Christ, and that a majority of Americans go to church almost every Sunday. Yet you never see people on television shows praying or talking about the things of God or going to church. When someone is presented as clearly religious, he or she is usually a fanatic in the bad sense of the word who is unloving and overbearing at best or a crazed killer who thinks he hears God telling him to murder people at worst.

Such is the picture television usually gives us of religion in general and Christianity in particular. It either ignores them altogether, or it shows them to be extremely abnormal. And neither is accurate.

How should you respond to television? First, realizing its potential impact, resolve that you are going to control it in your personal and family life rather than allow it unlimited access to your time.

Think carefully about what you intend to watch and what you let your children watch, and evaluate whether a given program is likely to have an overall positive or negative impact on your lives. Don't just turn on the set and let the television programmers bring the material of *their* choice into your home. Learn to say no to shows that look interesting but that are likely to do more harm than good in the long run to your spiritual health.

Don't use the television as a babysitter. If your children need to be occupied while you do other things around the house, get them books, games, and other toys that will challenge their minds and keep them active—and screen these carefully, too. When your children do watch TV, watch it with them as much as possible, and discuss what you're seeing in terms of its realism and the values that are being presented.

Best of all, do things with your family away from the television. Talk together, walk together, play together, wash the car or rake the leaves together, go on picnics or to museums together. Life is full of exciting and fulfilling activities that will build your family, and many of them cost nothing but time and a little effort.

Finally, don't sit back in silence and tolerate offensive television programming. In courteous but clear language, make your feelings known to your local stations and to the network programmers, as well as to the Federal Communications Commission. You might also want to contact the National Federation for Decency in Tupelo, Mississippi, for other ideas about how to influence television for the good. The Federation has, for instance, led effective consumer boycotts against advertisers who tend to support objectionable shows.

The Scourge of Pornography

When enjoyed by a husband and wife together, sex is one of God's most pleasant gifts. I am not against sex, and I certainly don't think it is somehow bad or evil. Just the opposite is true. It's wonderful! Indeed, it is one of God's presents to the human race.

I have no doubt, however, that soon after sin came into the world in the Garden of Eden, men and women began to corrupt

God's gift of sex and use it outside marriage and in unnatural ways that God had not intended. Paul speaks about some of these in Romans 1. Prostitution is often called "the world's oldest profession," and while that's probably not quite true—Adam, after all, was a farmer before the Fall—it's probably close to it.

In our day, sexual sin and sexual crime are more rampant than ever. And they are helped along by the relatively recent plague of pornography. Now, pornography has probably been around almost as long as written language. But until the last few decades, there was a common feeling among civilized people that pornography was wrong, and there wasn't a great deal of it that was widely available. There were also strict laws against it, and they were enforced with some vigor by the authorities.

But today, we're flooded with pornography, and the prevailing attitude is that it's OK if—and here's that phrase again—"no one gets hurt." What consenting adults or individuals do or look at in the privacy of their homes is nobody else's business, we're told. The problem, however, is that this is not *God's* attitude, and people are being hurt by pornography.

Some of the problems with pornography are obvious. For one thing, it degrades the gift of sex God gave us. It makes sex into something dirty. It divorces sex from marital love and makes it into nothing more than what animals do. It also degrades women, portraying them as objects whose sole mission in life is to give sensual pleasure to men. And most disgusting of all, much of it now degrades children as well, presenting them as sex objects for the pleasure of sick-minded adults.

For all these reasons, pornography is bad in and of itself. But it also corrupts the lives of those who make it and those who look at it. Imagine what a woman or a man who "stars" in those magazines and films must feel like and think of herself or himself. And the children who are made to perform in "kiddie porn" no doubt will carry emotional, psychological, and in some cases physical scars for the rest of their lives.

And what about the person who looks at pornography? Proverbs 23:7 says, "For as he thinks in his heart, so is he." In other words, what you fill your mind with and allow it to dwell on shapes you as a person. If we feed a polluted view of sex into our minds with pornography, our own perspective on sex will soon be polluted too. And this is what inevitably happens to all who feed their minds a steady diet of pornography.

As bad as that is, it's not the end of the story about what pornography does to the person who views it regularly. The U. S. Attorney General's Commission on Pornography concluded what common sense should have told us long ago: Many of those who commit sexual crimes like rape are heavy "users" of pornography, and there appears to be a causal connection. In other words, while looking at pornography alone won't lead a person to commit a crime, it may well contribute to the decision to do so. As I said earlier, pornography cheapens women and presents them as nothing more than objects whose purpose is to please men sexually. This realization has many women's groups as well as law enforcement officials more concerned than ever about the plague of pornography.

The major argument used by the producers and sellers of pornography in their defense is that it is protected by the free speech provision of the first amendment to the Constitution. However, courts at all levels have said this is not the case with legally obscene materials, and there are laws on the books everywhere that attempt to regulate pornography. All that's lacking are people who are concerned enough to get involved, to say no to the pornographers, and to take intelligent, legal action to stem the flood. If you want more information on this important subject, I would encourage you to read *The Mind Polluters* by Jerry Kirk (Thomas Nelson Publishers).

Among the things Kirk suggests you do in response to pornography are to speak or write to the managers of local stores where you do business and that sell such material. Let them know that you find these materials offensive and would feel better about patronizing their stores if you knew such magazines were no longer there. Likewise, contact your local law enforcement officials and encourage them to pursue antipornography cases vigorously. Write letters to the editors of your local newspapers. Be persistent in your efforts along these lines; don't expect drastic change in your community just because you write one letter. But the battle can be won if we take the effort.

James Dobson, one of the commissioners of the U. S. Attorney General's Commission on Pornography, said, "America could rid itself of hard-core pornography in 18 months if the recommendations offered [by the Commission] are implemented. . . . But that will occur *only* if American citizens demand action from their government. Nothing short of a public outcry will motivate our slumbering representatives to defend community standards of decency."

The Crime of Abortion

I have deliberately chosen to call abortion a crime because I believe emphatically that despite what the United States Supreme Court says, there is a Higher Authority who insists abortion always has been, is still, and forever will be a crime because it is murder. I recognize that many Christians of good will are not so sure of this, and some even disagree. I am neither a doctor nor a theologian, and I don't claim to have any new insights on the subject. But after studying the Word of God, I have developed some powerful convictions and believe this is another subject about which God's servants should be speaking boldly.

My beliefs concerning abortion are based on the understanding that God is the giver of life, that a new life is created at the moment of conception in the mother's womb, and that we have no right to destroy an innocent human life. As Job asked rhetorically, "In whose hand is the life of every living thing, and the breath of all mankind?" (12:10). The obvious implied answer is God Almighty. Isaiah the prophet described the Lord as "He who formed you from the womb" (44:24).

Probably the best-known passage of Scripture that shows God as the Creator of each individual is Psalm 139:13–16:

For You have formed my inward parts; You have covered me in my mother's womb. I will praise You, for I am fearfully and wonderfully made; marvelous are Your works, and that my soul knows very well. My frame was not hidden from You, when I was made in secret, and skillfully wrought in the lowest parts of the earth. Your eyes saw my substance, being yet unformed. And in Your book they all were written, the days fashioned for me, when as yet there were none of them.

God wonderfully makes the unborn child in the mother's womb, and He even knows what the future will hold for the person He is fashioning. I recognize that this passage is not meant as a scientific statement, but its basic point—that God gives life and forms the unborn child into the baby who will be born if allowed to do so—is entirely accurate.

One of the arguments often used by the so-called pro-choice advocates is that the unborn is only a fetus that represents "potential" life, and that it is not a fully human person until it is viable—that is, until it is able to survive outside the womb. Until then, they say, the fetus is only a part of the mother, a group of cells growing inside her with which she can do as she pleases. Using this criterion, they conclude that the fetus is not a child until late (at least six months) in a pregnancy, and that abortion is therefore permissible at least up to the point of viability.

I wonder, however, why the point at which an individual is a separate person apart from the mother is identified as the time of fetal viability. What vital transformation takes place at the time of fetal viability such that before, abortion was permissible, but now we have to think twice about it? What is now present in the fetus that wasn't there before? In terms of the nature of the child—what he will look like, what his basic personality will be like, what his inborn talents and interests will be, in short, his basic humanity and individuality—there's nothing present at the point of viability that was not present at the moment of conception, when the father's sperm joined the mother's egg to create a new, unique person who is part of each parent and yet separate from both.

The choice of the point of viability as the time when the fetus becomes a true child is arbitrary and without foundation. There is no logical reason for not pushing back the point of new personhood to the moment of conception. At the very least, we should agree with President Reagan when he observed that since we can't identify precisely when the fetus becomes a "person," however we define that, and since it certainly can't be proved that this *doesn't* happen at conception, should we not give the benefit of the doubt to the innocent child? My emphatic answer and my plea to our world is that yes, indeed, we should give the benefit to the unborn.

Again, make your views known to your senators and representatives at both the state and national levels. And once again, be courteous but clear and persistent.

I also believe that if we're going to stand against abortion, we have a further responsibility to provide alternatives to women who are pregnant and don't want the children they're carrying. This means counseling and encouragement, medical help, financial aid, and assistance in placing children for adoption once they are born. All these services must be offered in love and without condemnation.

If you want to know more about what can be done and you want to be further challenged by the need, I would encourage you to read Jerry Falwell's book *If I Should Die before I Wake*. I certainly admire Jerry Falwell's courage in standing up and speaking out in those areas where he believes God has called him to do so. In that respect, he is a model for all believers, and I recommend his book because space and the scope of this book prevent a fuller treatment of this important subject.

Sharing God's Love for the Poor

Finally, the child of God who has committed himself to being a servant of God should boldly proclaim a courageous message about an issue that is dear to the heart of God: an ongoing concern for world hunger and for the poor generally. I suspect that this problem is almost as old as the human race, and yet it is very much a contemporary problem.

There can be no doubt about the size of the problem of poverty and hunger in the world. Our television screens have been filled with tragic pictures from Ethiopia and other African nations, and yet there is also continuing hunger in India, Bangladesh, Mexico, and many other developing nations.

I have personally seen the wretchedness of the poor and hungry in places like Calcutta, India, as well as the cruelty of evil people who exploit the destitute in these places for their own gain—such as when children are deliberately mutilated to make them more pitiable beggars, and then what they are given is taken from them by their masters.

Nor can there be any doubt about God's concern for the poor and His desire to see us involved in helping to meet their needs. When He gave the Old Testament law, God told the people of Israel:

> If there is among you a poor man of your brethren, within any of the gates in your land which the Lord your God is giving you, you shall not harden your heart nor shut your hand from your poor brother, but you shall open your hand wide to him. . . . For the poor will never cease from the land; therefore I command you, saying, "You shall open your hand wide to your brother, to your poor and your needy, in your land" (Deut. 15:7-8, 11).

Likewise 1 John 3:17-18 says, "But whoever has this world's goods, and sees his brother in need, and shuts up his heart from him, how does the love of God abide in Him? My little children, let us not love in word or in tongue, but in deed and in truth." In a similar vein, the apostle James asked this rhetorical question: "If a brother or sister is naked and destitute of daily food, and one of you says to them, 'Depart in peace, be warmed and filled,' but you do not give them the things which are needed for the body, what does it profit?" (2:15-16).

Perhaps the strongest statement about our responsibility toward those who are poor and hungry comes from Jesus in the form of a promise:

> Then the King will say to those on His right hand, "Come, you blessed of My Father, inherit the kingdom prepared for you from the foundation of the world: for I was hungry and you gave Me

food; I was thirsty and you gave Me drink; I was a stranger and you took Me in; I was naked and you clothed Me; I was sick and you visited Me; I was in prison and you came to Me." Then the righteous will answer Him, saying, "Lord, when did we see You hungry and feed You, or thirsty and give You drink? When did we see You a stranger and take You in, or naked and clothe You? Or when did we see You sick, or in prison, and come to You?" And the King will answer and say to them, "Assuredly, I say to you, inasmuch as you did it to one of the least of these My brethren, you did it to Me" (Matt. 25:34–40).

He then went on to warn that those who refused to help "the least of these" would be turning their backs on Jesus Himself (see vv. 41–46).

Compassion for the poor and hungry must be an important issue for God's children. This is not surprising when we realize how much God loves every individual. He loves each person in a deep and practical way, and so should we. Out of a godly love and a desire to do the work of evangelism, we who claim the name of Christ should be doing more than anyone else to meet the needs and alleviate the suffering of the poor and hungry. We care because we follow the One Who cares supremely, Who takes upon Himself the problems and the pains of all men and women.

I am happy to say that there are many charitable Christian organizations, both here and abroad, that do a tremendous amount of good in the name of the Lord. But I wonder if we here in the richest nation in the world couldn't do even more. I know of very few people who give to the point of sacrificing even a single meal so that the truly hungry may eat. I urge you to give prayerful consideration to what you can do to contribute both to overseas relief work and to relief work in your own community. This latter might mean you should become involved in your church's benevolence program, a local food bank, or a downtown rescue mission.

God's servants should be in the forefront of such work. It is to our shame when non-Christian people or governmental agencies have more compassion than we. Or, looking at the matter positively, who more than a Christian has a good motivation to reach out to those in need? We do it, as with all our service, out of gratitude to the God who has lovingly made us His children, and as a way to share that love with others.

A Courageous Message

The six issues I've discussed in this chapter—the deity of Jesus Christ, the inspiration of Scripture, the influence of television, the scourge of pornography, the crime of abortion, and sharing God's love for the poor—are among those that I believe are especially important in our time, and I am convinced that God wants His servants to speak out boldly about them.

I doubt that you personally will have an opportunity to make a significant statement on all these issues, but you should be prepared to proclaim a courageous message as God gives you the opportunity. Indeed, you should look for and seize opportunities to speak a courageous message. If you'll do that, you'll enjoy the warmth of the Master's smile.

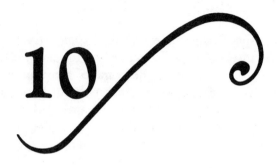

"NO" IS A
NECESSARY WORD

AUTHOR AND PASTOR Stephen Brown tells of talking one time with the Youth for Christ director in his area about a local ministry in which both had been asked to become involved. Both of them felt that the ministry was one they would like to support, but they both had many commitments already and were struggling with whether they could take on this responsibility in addition to their existing duties.

Brown said to the YFC director, "Don't you sometimes feel guilty because you aren't more involved?"

The man answered, "No, I don't. That isn't my ministry; that is someone else's. I have been called to work with kids."[1]

What the YFC director was saying is that when you have discerned God's clear call on your life, you sometimes have to say no to other good opportunities in order to do your best in the ministry God has already given you. In saying that, this YFC worker was absolutely right. "No" is a necessary word if you're to be an effective servant. And because it's not easy to say no—because the easy and popular thing is to give in to the expectations of others and say yes—because it takes real strength and resolve to stand firm in turning down a request for help—*many times that word "no" is itself the courageous message God is calling you to speak.*

God calls each of us as individuals. He gives us unique spiritual gifts and calls us individually to various kinds of ministries. We're not all supposed to be doing the exact same things, and we don't all have to look or talk alike, either. Yet the church today is plagued by busyness and is full of worn-out Christians. This is because we do not recognize our uniqueness, but we all try to be involved in too many ministries. We have not learned how to say no, and we have our priorities in the wrong order. You need to understand that it's okay—even necessary—to say no to others, including fellow servants of God, when that's what it takes to keep your priorities in order and your health intact.

Charles Spurgeon, the great British preacher of the last century, was also a teacher of pastoral students. At that time, Latin was the "official" language of higher education. It was the language of the earliest printed Bibles, and it was essential that students at the university level be fluent in it. But Spurgeon was fond of telling his students, "Learn to say no. It will do you more good than Latin." He knew the truth I'm trying to convey to you now.

Billy Graham is one of the busiest men alive, and certainly the busiest man I know personally. Most of what he does when he's working is related to his work as an evangelist. You may hear in the news of his meeting with government leaders, speaking to one group or another, serving on the board of directors of a ministry, or being engaged in some activity other than preaching in a crusade. He does all those things, but the largest percentage of Billy's time is spent in activities directly connected to his calling as an evangelist. He knows that getting too involved in other things—

no matter how good they may be—would take him away from his primary calling more than he can afford if he's to give it his best. When he's not preaching, he may be writing sermons, praying for upcoming meetings and crusades, or meeting with local crusade organizers. Mass evangelism is his calling as a servant of God, and after his personal relationship with the Lord and his relationships with his family, that remains his top priority.

Most of us aren't as busy as Billy Graham. But we are extremely busy in our own right, and I'm sure you have more opportunities for involvement than your schedule and energies can accommodate. So what do you do? You have to learn to say yes to what's most important and no to the rest, no matter how good those things may be. Charles Spurgeon learned that lesson, Billy Graham has learned it, and you and I need to learn it also if we haven't already.

Why Saying No Takes Courage

It's easy for me to say you need to learn to say no, but it's not so easy for you to actually do it when your church's Christian education director calls and asks you to help with Vacation Bible School, work with the high school youth group, or teach a Sunday school class—no matter how busy you may already be in a ministry that you believe is God's primary calling on your service. It's not easy to say no when your pastor asks you to represent your congregation in a denominational meeting to formulate a statement about the inerrancy of Scripture or help serve meals to elderly people in your community who can't cook for themselves. Why is it so hard?

For one thing, we're concerned about how the people to whom we say no will react. We care what people think about us, and we're afraid that fellow Christians who hear we turned down a request for service will think we're selfish or lazy or just not very spiritual. And, of course, the more important the person doing the asking is to us, the harder it is to say no because the more we care about his opinion of us. It's a lot easier to turn down a fellow parishioner than your senior pastor.

In this situation, however, we need to keep God and His calling clearly in mind, because it's more important that we please Him and have His favor than that we please any other person. Think about how *He'll* feel if you give less than your best effort to your relationship with Him, your family, or your primary calling because you couldn't say no to some other demand on your time.

On one occasion Peter and the other apostles said, "We ought to obey God rather than men" (Acts 5:29). Although their situation was somewhat different—they were responding to an order from the authorities in Jerusalem not to preach the gospel—what they said applies equally well whenever you're asked to do something that would diminish your effectiveness in your unique, primary calling. The person asking may not realize your predicament, and you can try to explain, but the "bottom line" is that you need to be most concerned about pleasing God, regardless of who is asking you to do something else.

I know that it takes guts to say no sometimes. And that's why sometimes the courageous message God wants you to give is to say no to the people you'd most like to please. That's not easy, but it is necessary.

Another reason we don't like to say no is that when we do, we tend to feel guilty, as though we're turning down not just the person doing the asking but also God. Many of the people who ask for our service know that, and often they're not above trying to manipulate us with that guilt. But remember that if you're a child of God, you're a forgiven person because you are covered by Christ's righteousness. God isn't going to stop loving you and throw you out of His family if you turn down any particular responsibility. As a forgiven servant, you should never allow anyone to make you feel guilty or to manipulate you by doing so. To permit that is to put yourself back under the bondage from which Jesus freed you!

Moreover, God is sovereign and will achieve His purpose. He wants you to be involved in His work and has commanded you to do so, but whether you ever say yes to any service for Him or not, His purposes will be accomplished. You don't ever need to feel guilty about saying no to a request for your involvement in a ministry for fear that if you don't do the job, it won't get done. You may miss out on a blessing God wanted you to receive, but I assure you that if God is in the ministry and wants that work to get done, He'll see to it that the work is accomplished whether you do it yourself or fly off to Timbuktu and leave the task to someone else.

Another reason why it takes courage to say no is that we like to feel indispensable. We like to think that if we were to leave the scene tomorrow, our homes, offices, and churches would fall apart. It takes honesty and courage to admit to ourselves—let alone to others—that we are dispensable after all and that God can get His work done without us if need be, thank you very much. Humility isn't popular today, and it requires more courage than foolish bragging does.

Proclaiming a Courageous Message Effectively

In this section, we've seen that God calls all His servants to speak a courageous message, and we've looked at some of the issues He wants us to address today. We've considered, too, that whereas God gives us different burdens for particular issues, for all of us the courageous message sometimes must be the simple but very difficult word "No."

To serve God most effectively in this area, we must analyze carefully the primary ministry to which He is calling us, as well as those one or two issues with which He would have us be most involved. A great danger is that we'll try to do too many things, however good, at once, and end up giving less than our best effort to all of them.

We also need to learn to draw on God's strength, as described in chapter 4, for the wisdom, courage, and persistence without which we cannot succeed. If we try to get across any message on God's behalf in our own strength, our motives or our methods will be wrong, and in either case we'll fail.

Remember, too, that whenever we represent God in any capacity, our speech and conduct should be marked by love and forgiveness. In the heat of conflict over one of the issues Christians should address today or when we express our firm no to a request for our involvement, it's easy to become unloving very quickly, to be defensive and hostile. But that is not the way of mature servants of God.

The Lord calls us today to proclaim a courageous message, just as He called Jeremiah so many years ago. This is an important part of what it means to be His servant and so to walk in the lasting joy He has promised to those who follow Him.

---

1. Stephen Brown, *If God Is in Charge* (Nashville: Thomas Nelson, 1983), p. 95.

Part IV

A CHALLENGING

PURPOSE

THE GREATEST PURPOSE
IN THE WORLD

JUST SEVENTY-SIX YEARS AGO, the people of the Hmar tribe in northeastern India were brutal, warring headhunters. When they won a battle, they would decapitate their victims and hang the heads over the doors of their bamboo huts. In a single raid on a British tea plantation, they took five hundred heads.

Today, however, the Hmar are a far different people. At least 95 percent are Christians, and they worship in more than two hundred churches. They've sent five hundred missionaries to other, surrounding tribes. Furthermore, 85 percent can read and write, which is an amazing statistic in India. They learn at eighty-eight church-sponsored elementary schools, seven junior high schools, and four high schools. They also have a good hospital that is staffed by doctors and nurses from their own tribe. Their per capita income is much higher than the Indian national average.

What accounts for this incredible transformation in the Hmar people? It is the dedication of one Welsh missionary who had a challenging purpose and the power of God through His Word, the Bible. Watkin Roberts was a chemist when a revival swept through his part of Wales. His heart was stirred, and he gained a new desire to serve God. After reading a British soldier's account of an encounter with the Hmars, Roberts felt God calling him to take the Bible to them.

When he arrived in India in 1910, Roberts was warned against entering Hmar territory by the British agent for the area. So Roberts found some Lushais, who spoke the same language as the Hmars, and began translating the Bible into the Lushai language.

When a Christian woman in England sent Roberts a gift of five pounds—a sizable amount of money in those days—he used the money to print a few hundred copies of the Gospel of John in Lushai and sent them by runner to the chiefs of every Hmar village.

When the chief in the village of Senvon received a copy, he was curious to know what it said. A literate Lushai tribesman was there at the time and read the Gospel of John to him. But the Lushai couldn't explain what the term "born again" in John 3 meant, and so he suggested that the chief invite the translator, Roberts, to come himself.

As soon as Roberts received the invitation, he asked the British agent for permission to go. But the agent refused, telling him, "When I go in there, I take a hundred soldiers along for protection. I can't spare a single soldier for you. That invitation is an invitation to have your head lopped off." Roberts was not about to miss such an opportunity, however, so he found an interpreter and went to Senvon anyway.

The rest, as they say, is history. With the help of the interpreter, Roberts found a way to explain the gospel of God's grace in a way the Hmars could understand. That day, the chief and four other

Hmars said they wanted to make peace with the great God of the Bible. Afterward, Roberts returned to the British post where he lived. For his efforts to evangelize the Hmars, the other British in the area labeled him a troublemaker. The British agent had him whipped and ordered him to leave.

What God had started through Watkin Roberts, however, was not about to be stopped. Before long, Hmar preachers were traveling out from that first village by foot and canoe to every part of the Hmar country, telling people to accept God's sacrifice for the forgiveness of their sins. Churches were started in almost every Hmar village, and thousands of people accepted God's salvation with joy.

As the Hmars were converted, their lives were transformed. They had been used to fighting, drinking, and living in fear of evil spirits. Now they had a new reason to live and a desire to work hard and build schools for their children. The result of this was a radical transformation of their lifestyle. The Hmars are truly one of the great success stories in the history of Christian missions— and it all started with one person who had a challenging purpose from God.

At the Heart of God's Work

When God called Jeremiah to be His servant, He gave Jeremiah a clear call to service, said that He expected Jeremiah to lead a clean life, and put words into Jeremiah's mouth in the form of a courageous message. God then said to Jeremiah, "You shall go to all to whom I sent you." God gave Jeremiah a challenging purpose. And just as the other principles are important elements in bringing lasting joy into the life of God's servants, so also is the challenge of God to go to those to whom He sends us. God gives each of His servants a challenging purpose by expecting each to be involved in evangelism—in seeing people's lives transformed through an encounter with the person of Jesus Christ.

Have you ever wondered what your life is all about, what purpose you could have for living that would give you a good reason to get out of bed every morning? Have you had a growing desire to serve God, but you also want excitement? There ought to be joy in any kind of Christian service, but as far as I'm concerned, nothing beats the thrill of evangelism. Believe me, I haven't dedicated my life to this work because I find it dull or a waste of my time. And if you really want excitement, try to top the experiences of Watkin Roberts!

Now, since I'm an evangelist and I work with Billy Graham, you probably expected me to talk about evangelism sooner or later. But please don't dismiss what I'm saying just because you expected me to bring up the subject. Both from the Bible and from my own experience, I am absolutely convinced that evangelism is a part of God's purpose for every Christian, and that it truly is the most fulfilling and exciting work in which anyone could be involved. You'll recall that I started my work as an evangelist with great reluctance, but I now consider myself to be the most fortunate of people.

Why is evangelistic work so exciting and rewarding? It's because evangelism is at the very center of God's heart and of His purpose for His people in every age. When God first called Abraham out of Ur of the Chaldees, He said to him, "I will bless you and make your name great; and you shall be a blessing . . . and in you all the families of the earth shall be blessed" (Gen. 12:2–3). When God was first establishing a people for Himself, He made it clear that He intended for them to be a blessing to others—in this case, He was referring especially to the fact that Jesus, the Savior of the world, would come from the nation Abraham was founding.

Many years later, as the people of Israel were about to enter the Promised Land after the Exodus from Egypt and the wandering in the wilderness, Moses reminded them of one of the most important reasons for the laws and regulations God had given them to observe:

Therefore be careful to observe them [God's laws]; for this is your wisdom and your understanding in the sight of the peoples who will hear all these statutes, and say, "Surely this great nation is a wise and understanding people." For what great nation is there that has God so near to it, as the Lord our God is to us, for whatever reason we may call upon Him? And what great nation is there that has such statutes and righteous judgments as are in all this law which I set before you this day? (Deut. 4:6-8).

By following God's laws and thus living righteously, the people of Israel were to be an example, a witness, to the surrounding nations. They were to make those people aware of the holiness of the one true God.

In the New Testament as well, we see God's desire to have people reconciled to Himself and His willingness to take the initiative to bring that about. John 3:16 tells us "God so loved the world that He gave His only begotten Son . . . ." We read in 2 Peter 3:9 that the Lord "is longsuffering toward us, not willing that any should perish, but that all should come to repentance." Paul wrote to Timothy that God "desires all men to be saved and to come to the knowledge of the truth" (1 Tim. 2:4).

It is clear from Scripture that God loves us, that He has offered the sacrifice necessary to pay the price for our sins and to make our reconciliation with Him possible, and that seeing people respond in faith to His love is His greatest desire for everyone everywhere. Since these things are true, what work could be closer to God's heart, and what kind of service could be more exciting than evangelism?

Every time a person is born spiritually into God's family, we are privileged to witness a miracle. By faith we ask God to forgive us, and He does. It is a marvelous wonder when a baby is born physically into this world, but it is a far greater miracle when a person is reborn spiritually.

As I sit on the platform of the Billy Graham crusades night after night and see thousands of people respond to God's invitation to salvation, I am often overcome with emotion at the wonder of it. I have to bow my head and fight to keep from crying like a baby. That thrill is what makes it such a wonderful privilege to be an evangelist and what keeps me going day after day. Truly, there is no other work in the world that I'd rather do.

The Biblical Command

The challenging purpose of evangelism is a gift God gives to all His servants, not just to those who are full-time evangelists. We should all be involved in evangelistic work, first, because it's obviously something very close to the heart of God. As His children and servants, we should want to be a part of anything that's so important to Him. Second, it's an exciting, rewarding work that brings great purpose and fulfillment into our lives.

But there's also a third very important reason for being involved in evangelistic work: Evangelism is something God has clearly *commanded* in His Word that all of us should do. To refuse is to rebel against His authority. To obey is to bring joy into your life.

You're probably familiar with some of the biblical passages that give the call to evangelism. In Acts 1:8, just before the resurrected Jesus ascended into heaven, He said to His disciples, "You shall receive power when the Holy Spirit has come upon you; and you shall be witnesses to Me in Jerusalem, and in all Judea and Samaria, and to the end of the earth." This was both a command and a statement of fact.

Jesus told them they would be witnesses first in Jerusalem. That was the local area where they lived. For comparison, if you live in Chicago, your "Jerusalem"—the first place where you should be a witness—is right there in Chicago.

Next, the disciples were to go to Judea and Samaria, the parts of their country outside the immediate area. Jerusalem was actually the major city in the region of Judea. Comparing this with the person living in Chicago, "Judea" would be the state of Illinois, of which Chicago is the largest city, and "Samaria" would be the rest of the United States.

Finally, Jesus' followers were to go "to the end of the earth"— anywhere there were people who had not yet heard the good news of the gospel. This part of the command needs no modern comparison. Whether you live in Chicago or someplace else, you are still under commission to go wherever Jesus is not yet known.

Another familiar passage about evangelism is Matthew 28:18-20, the Great Commission. Jesus said, "All authority has been given to Me in heaven and on earth. Go therefore and make disciples of all the nations, baptizing them in the name of the Father and of the Son and of the Holy Spirit, teaching them to observe all things that I have commanded you; and lo, I am with you always, even to the end of the age." That's pretty clear and straightforward. We're to go, make disciples, baptize, and teach.

Lest there be any misunderstanding, let me emphasize again that these commands of Jesus were meant for *all* His disciples, both then and now. If you're a child of God through faith in Jesus Christ, they apply to you just as much as they do to me. Evangelism isn't just the work of missionaries, pastors, and full-time evangelists. It is part of God's challenging purpose for all His children.

I realize that for many Christians evangelism isn't easy, and the thought of witnessing to a nonbeliever can be a frightening prospect. Some people have more naturally outgoing personalities, but, if you do not, there are many ways to be involved in the work of evangelism and God will use you in evangelistic work in a way that will fit your personality. But no Christian can ignore the work of evangelism and be faithful to the commands of the Lord. As Manford Gutzke wrote, "The Christian is given the task of winning souls to God. Most believers would be glad if churches would do that: if others would reach out and bring people in. But this is the task given to each believer."[1]

With that understanding, let's look at the Great Commission again and notice a few things about it. First, we see that we're to go in God's power, not our own. "All authority has been given to me. . . . Go" (vv. 18-19). We discussed this at length in chapter 4, so I won't dwell on it now, but we need to be reminded that apart from Him we can do nothing (see John 15:4-8).

Second, note the program Jesus gave us to follow. We're to make disciples, which means leading people to Christ, or evangelism. We're then to baptize them, which means, among other things, bringing them into the fellowship of a local church. And we're also to teach them to obey God, which means training and building them up to spiritual maturity. As Paul said in Colossians 1:28, "Him [Jesus] we preach, warning every man and teaching every man in all wisdom, that we may present every man perfect [mature] in Christ Jesus." The responsibility of evangelism, therefore, does not end when someone comes forward to accept Christ. Rather, the responsibility of the servant who is fulfilling the Great Commission is only beginning.

Finally, Jesus promised that He would be with us: "and lo, I am with you always, even to the end of the age" (Matt. 28:20). We have the assurance that wherever we go and whatever we do in His service, we're not alone. He is there with us, and from that promise we can draw great hope, comfort, and courage.[2]

The apostle Paul summed up well both the view we should have of ourselves and the message we should present to the world: "Therefore we are ambassadors for Christ, as though God were pleading through us: we implore you on Christ's behalf, be reconciled to God" (2 Cor. 5:20).

Pith Helmets, Anyone?

The biblical mandate to be involved in evangelism is clear. But just what might that mean in your life? What specifically would God have you do? God would have some be involved in full-time missions or evangelistic work. This certainly isn't true of every Christian, but the need is great, and God is still calling many to this kind of life. And missionary work doesn't necessarily mean preaching. There are other types of work that missionaries do and for which you might be better suited or gifted by God.

Suppose you're a doctor, a teacher, a printer, an administrator, a nurse, an accountant, a photographer, or a mechanic. If you're willing to offer your skills in missions work, there's almost certainly a place for you in full-time service, either in a faraway place like Africa, Asia, Europe, Indonesia, or here in America. In the past few years, we have also seen a relatively new phenomenon called the short-term missionary. It used to be that a missionary calling always meant a lifetime commitment. Now, however, many Christians go for just a year or two to do a specific project. Some even go for just a few months or weeks.

Short-term missions is a good thing because it gets many people involved who are not prepared to give the rest of their lives to missions for one reason or another. By giving their time and using their particular skills, these people also get work done that full-time missionaries would find difficult if not impossible. And if you ever take part in such a project, even if only for a week, I guarantee you'll be a changed person.

For all these reasons, I would encourage you to take part in short-term missions if full-time service is not your calling. On the other hand, if you think God may be asking you to become a missionary, a short-term experience can help you evaluate your abilities, interest, and dedication more realistically.

Let me repeat again, however, that the need for full-time, lifelong missionaries is still great. There are still many peoples in our world who have not been introduced to the gospel of Jesus Christ. And there are areas of the world that have had the gospel for many years but, like much of Western Europe, have grown spiritually cold. They need missionaries to help revitalize their churches. Don't think the day of missions is past. Be sensitive to the leading of the Holy Spirit in your life in case He should want you to go.

One of the most important reasons lifelong missionaries are needed is that it takes time to learn the language and customs of foreign people, and to establish relationships with native people once you arrive in your place of service. Relationships are the key to effective evangelism. Therefore, a missionary needs to spend time with people so they can see that Christ is real in his life and that his actions are consistent with his words of Christian love. Relationships like these take time to build.

If God is leading you to devote your life to missionary service, you should become active now in your local church and its evangelistic efforts if you're not already. This will give you good experience and a chance to evaluate your aptitude for such work. Besides that, if you find you don't really have an evangelist's hunger for souls or the ability to meet new people and establish relationships with them, you need to seriously question your call. Finding yourself on a foreign mission field won't change your heart or create new talents in you overnight. If you don't already have the desire and abilities of a missionary here, you're likely to be a miserably unhappy missionary when you land in a foreign country. Crossing the ocean won't make you a missionary and going to a theological seminary won't make you a preacher. If you are going to be a missionary, you should be a missionary now and if you are going to be a preacher, you should tell others about the gospel of Jesus Christ now.

Do you want excitement? Do you want to be at the heart of God's work in this world? Do you want a cause that's worth living—and dying—for? Then I submit that you should look at the work of a missionary and consider whether God would have you give your life to it.

Evangelism at Home

I know that God's will for most Christians does not include full-time missions work, either here or abroad. But the Great Commission is a command given to all Christians nonetheless. All of God's servants are to have the challenging purpose of proclaiming the gospel. There are many ways in which you can be an active part of world missions without leaving your town, as we'll see in the next chapter. But in addition, you are called to be an evangelist to the people around you right where you are.

Just as a missionary should build relationships in a foreign country by demonstrating a quality of life characterized by love and truthfulness based on his relationship with Jesus Christ, so all of God's people everywhere should demonstrate such a life. When people look at our lives, they should see the joy and love that rightfully belong to those who serve a risen and loving Lord. Christians should be among the people in every community who are most known for caring about others and being in the forefront of efforts to help those who need it. And when asked what motivates us, the answer should be "the love of God."

Jesus emphasized this truth when He said, "You are the light of the world. A city that is set on a hill cannot be hidden. Nor do they light a lamp and put it under a basket, but on a lampstand, and it gives light to all who are in the house. Let your light so shine before men, that they may see your good works and glorify your Father in heaven" (Matt. 5:14–16). Peter said that we should be ready to explain to people why we are caring and loving: "Be ready at any time to give a quiet and reverent answer to any man who wants a reason for the hope that you have within you" (1 Peter 3:15, *Phillips*).

Other people are looking for a reason to live, a worthwhile cause to motivate them to get up every morning. If we can show them a life full of love, hope, and kindness, a life that honors God and doesn't fall apart in difficult circumstances, they'll want to know how they can have the same quality of life.

An inventor once went to a banker to ask for financial backing for his new machine. The banker listened carefully to the inventor's explanation of the project and how the machine worked, and then he said, "Before I invest in your machine, I need to know whether the public will buy it. Do you have a working model?" The non-Christian world around us is asking the same thing of the church. We can talk all we want about our faith, but can we show them lives changed by Jesus Christ that "work," that are of such quality that they would want the same thing for themselves? If we can, people will "invest."

On the other hand, if our lives don't have a quality that attracts others, we can lose out on opportunities to be a part of what God is doing in reconciling people to Himself. A distraught man came to see his pastor one time. He told the pastor that a fellow worker had been involved in a terrible accident in which a pot of molten lead had fallen on him and covered a large part of his body. Another worker yelled, "Get a doctor, quick!"

But the injured man said, "It's too late for a doctor. Someone tell me about God and how to get to heaven!"

At this point the pastor said to the man in his office, "You could have told him how to be saved."

With tears in his eyes, the man replied, "That's the trouble,

Pastor. I couldn't because all the men I've worked beside year after year have never heard me speak up for Christ. They've never heard me pray, never heard me present a Christian point of view in any conversation, never heard me witness. What they have heard is my profaning His name and laughing with them at every off-color joke and story. What would they have thought if I had now tried to lead a man to Christ?"

Because this man had no better quality of life than the men around him, he realized he had given up any chance to reach them for Christ.

A wise person once said, "You are the only Bible some people will ever read." For that man in the factory, he was probably the only example some of his co-workers had of what the Christian life is like—if they even knew he was a believer. Or as Manford Gutzke put it, "Each Christian person is like a letter written to the community showing the gospel of Jesus Christ."[3] The question, then, is what kind of picture do you and I give the watching world of what the Christian life is all about? Living a life full of love, hope, and kindness is doing the work of an evangelist because you are showing the people with whom you come into contact that God is real and that a relationship with Him can make a difference in a person's life.

Let me suggest also that if you love the Lord and are walking closely with Him day by day, you will find yourself talking about Him as part of your everyday conversation. Have you ever noticed that if a subject really interests you—for example, your child's latest outstanding report card—you will think and talk about it a lot? The fact is that things that are important to us just naturally work their way into our conversation. This should be as true of our relationship with God as it is with any other subject.

I know this is easier and more natural for some than for others. If you have the gift of evangelism, you can use it even if evangelism is not your full-time work. Even though I'm convinced that all God's children are to be involved in the work of evangelism in some way, I don't want to wield a Christian cookie cutter, either, by suggesting you have to be like me or some other preacher. As

I've said throughout this book, you need to identify God's unique calling on your life and service and set your priorities accordingly.

But at the very least, all Christians should be involved in lifestyle evangelism such as I've been describing because God has given us the wonderful, exciting, challenging purpose of going to all to whom He sends us with the good news of Jesus Christ, whether He sends us across the street or across the ocean.

---

1. Manford George Gutzke, *Born to Serve*, pp. 118–19.
2. For a more complete discussion of the Great Commission, see Billy Graham, *A Biblical Standard for Evangelists* (Minneapolis: World Wide, 1984), pp. 23–30.
3. Gutzke, p. 123.

WHAT CAN
I DO?

HAVE YOU EVER BEEN in a situation where Christians heard of a need and wished they could do something to help, but for some reason they weren't able? So then someone in the group said, "Well, at least we can pray for them." And because we know it's good to pray for others and at least then we're doing *something* for the people in need, everybody jumps at that suggestion and a brief prayer is offered.

If you've been in a church for any length of time, you've probably experienced that kind of thing more than once. And of course it *is* good to pray for others. But when Christians in that situation say, "At least we can pray," it's obvious they don't have a very high opinion of prayer and think prayer really is the least they can do. Prayer is a last resort, the weak gesture you offer when you can't do anything else but you want to feel you "at least" did something. Such a perspective certainly doesn't come from the Bible or the great saints of ages past.

The Bible offers many examples of the power of prayer. For instance, the book of James says, "The earnest prayer of a righteous man has great power and wonderful results. Elijah was as completely human as we are, and yet when he prayed earnestly that no rain would fall, none fell for the next three and one-half years! Then he prayed again, this time that it would rain, and down it poured and the grass turned green and the gardens began to grow again" (5:16–18, TLB).

There was nothing weak about Elijah's prayers. He believed God was listening and would respond, and indeed He did. Prayer was also a central part of the daily activities of men like Daniel and Paul—and even the Lord Jesus Himself. They were all filled with the power of God as the result.

Likewise, Martin Luther declared, "I have so much business I cannot get on without spending three hours daily in prayer." John Wesley stated that "God does nothing but in answer to prayer," and he demonstrated that he really believed that by praying two hours every day. Author Richard Foster summarized the devotion to prayer of spiritual giants such as these by saying, "For these, and all those who have braved the depths of the interior life, to breathe was to pray."[1]

In 1983, the Billy Graham organization prepared *The Billy Graham Crusade Handbook* for distribution at the International Conference for Itinerant Evangelists that was held in Amsterdam, the Netherlands. It was written by Sterling Huston, our Director of North American Crusades, and in it Sterling captured well our attitude toward prayer as it relates to the work of evangelism. Speaking of preparations for a crusade, he wrote:

The most important step is prayer. The members of the Billy Graham Team are keenly aware that a successful Crusade can only come about through the blessing of God. Billy Graham has often said that there are three important elements in a Crusade—prayer, prayer, and prayer. A Crusade needs to be born in prayer, bathed in prayer, and built on prayer. If God does not bless in response to the prayers of His people, all human efforts will be fruitless. . . . Focus on prayer as the first priority in evangelism. People, methods, and materials are only instruments. It is through prayer that these instruments become effective by the empowering of the Holy Spirit.[2]

The Need for Senders

By now you may be thinking this is a chapter devoted entirely to the subject of prayer. It's not. Rather, it's directed to you who do not feel called to a life of full-time missionary service, showing what you can do to advance the cause of world evangelization right where you are.

The apostle Paul wrote, "How then shall they call on Him in whom they have not believed? And how shall they believe in Him of whom they have not heard? And how shall they hear without a preacher? [That's the evangelist or missionary.] And how shall they preach unless they are sent?" (Rom. 10:14–15). That's where you come in, as a sender. There are five things you can do right now where you are and without leaving home that will significantly advance the cause of world evangelization. The first and most important thing you can do is to pray, pray, pray. It's not the "least you can do"—it's more than anything else you could do.

God's missionaries and evangelists need your fervent, faith-filled prayers on their behalf. They need your prayers regularly. I can't tell you how many times I've heard stories of a missionary who was in some kind of difficulty but experienced a miraculous deliverance, only to learn later that at his very moment of need, the Lord had laid a special burden of prayer for that missionary on the heart of a believer in the missionary's home country. Truly, God works in answer to prayer.

How should you pray? Your prayers should be more than just

the "God bless all the missionaries" variety. You should learn all you can about the specific work, family, and needs of the missionaries for whom you want to pray. Get on their mailing lists so you can always have the latest news and prayer requests from them. And pray specifically for the needs and concerns they have. That way, when God answers those prayers, you'll be able to rejoice right along with the missionaries and their other "senders," and your own faith will be strengthened as well!

The great thing about prayer as a way of supporting the work of missions is that anyone can take part. You don't have to be rich, smart, young, old, or superspiritual to pray. God invites all His children to come into His presence in prayer, and that includes children, the elderly, the sick, the poor, and new Christians, too. Even if you think that all you can do is pray, you certainly should, because that's the best possible thing you *could* do.

A second way you can support missionaries is to write to them. If you've ever been away from home for any length of time—perhaps when you went away to college—you know how exciting it is to receive a letter from home. I have a friend whose aunt has a wonderful ministry of letter writing. Whenever her nieces or nephews first go to college, they find letters of encouragement and challenge waiting there. The letters let them know that their aunt cares for them and is praying for them. Your letter to a missionary can do the same thing. In God's providence, it might even arrive just when he's had a particularly difficult experience and is badly in need of some encouragement.

What would you say in a letter to a missionary? If the individual or family are personal acquaintances, you'll have common friends and experiences you can write about. Like the rest of us, missionaries want to hear the latest news about people they know and care for, and about what's happening in their home churches.

If you haven't previously met the missionaries to whom you are writing, introduce yourself and your family to them. They would love to meet you through correspondence. Enclose pictures of your family. Tell them what God is teaching you through your experiences and His Word. Assure them that you remember them in your prayers regularly. Feel free to ask them questions about their work, about the people to whom they're ministering, and about the country in which they're living.

Don't forget to let your children take part in writing to missionaries too. Make it a family affair. You can include their questions and comments in your letters, but encourage them to write their own. Chances are they would love to do it, and I know the missionaries would be thrilled to receive their letters.

A third way you can advance the cause of world evangelization is to take part in the missions activities of your local church. If your church has a missions committee, volunteer to be a part of it and help in any way you can. Many churches have an annual missions conference. Such an event offers lots of opportunities to serve in various ways.

If there's not much happening in your church regarding missions right now, perhaps God would have you to be the one to get things started. Tell your Sunday school class, your pastor, and your friends in the church about your excitement for missions. Relate to them some of the great stories about what's happening in missions right now. Ask the leaders of the congregation to pray and think about what God would have the church do about world missions. Remember that every great idea starts with one person whose enthusiasm sparks the interest of others.

Another way to support missionaries throughout the world is to let God use your home as a missions center. I know of at least two ways you can do this, and you'll probably come up with others if you give it a little thought.

Make your home available as a place where missionaries who are visiting your town can stay. These could be new missionaries who are visiting churches in your area to try to raise support, or they could be experienced missionaries who are home on furlough and are reporting to the congregations that already back them financially.

If your church belongs to a denomination that sends missionaries, or if your church works with one or more of the independent mission agencies, you can make your willingness known directly to the mission headquarters, and you should also tell your pastor.

I'm sure he would be glad to pass the information along to the appropriate people, and he can then keep you in mind when missionaries visit your own church.

What do you have to offer these missionaries who stay in your home? Your friendship and fellowship, a comfortable bed, some good food, and maybe transportation around town. Believe me, all these gifts will be greatly appreciated.

And what will you get in return? Far more than you'll ever give. You'll gain the lasting friendship of some wonderful people, many of whom are among God's choicest and most dedicated servants. You'll learn a great deal about the work of missions and the places where the missionaries are serving, and both kinds of knowledge will expand your thinking and your interest in missions tremendously.

Perhaps the greatest benefit of all is that by inviting missionaries into your home, your children will be exposed to these fine people, and the impact could well change their lives. Children are fascinated by faraway places and people with different languages and customs, and they'll love to learn all they can from your guests. This exposure will give them an early interest in missions that will likely continue throughout their lives and may even inspire them to careers in missions themselves.

Another way of making your home a missions center is to start a missions club in your home. I know of several of these in Minnesota, and it would be wonderful if the concept spread across the country.

The basic idea is that you get together once a month with a few other people who share your interest in missions for an evening devoted to your common concern. You might start with a potluck dinner or some light refreshments. This gives you a chance to socialize a little and catch up on one another's lives.

Then you get down to business, which is a presentation by a visiting missionary or someone in your group who's done some research on a particular missionary, mission project, or country. You might also ask a professor from a local Christian college, a mission agency spokesperson, or someone else who is familiar with mission work to tell your group about such things as how a missionary who's translating the Bible into a foreign language works, why the term "hidden peoples" is so popular among missions professionals these days, how other countries like South Korea are now sending out missionaries (it's not just the Western world any more, praise God!), or why emphasis is being placed on training indigenous evangelists.

One word of caution is in order here, although I hate to have to say it. The fact is that missionary speakers have a reputation for being deadly dull, and unfortunately the reputation is too often well earned. If you get a few speakers like this in a row, it could kill the interest of your group. You should do a little research before inviting a speaker, and try to find as many enthusiastic speakers as you can. Your speaker does not have to be a great orator. But he should be genuinely excited about the work God is doing through him. His enthusiasm will be contagious, and your group will respond eagerly.

Also, you can make any speaker more effective by welcoming him warmly and letting him know he's among friends who are sincerely interested in him and his work. That will help relax him and encourage him to speak easily and frankly. Also urge him to describe his frustrations as well as his successes. He'll appreciate the chance to get down off the pedestal missionaries are so often put on and speak honestly about his work. That will give you a better picture of what's happening.

Encourage your speaker to give you very specific prayer requests: names of people to whom he's witnessing and names of local officials whose cooperation he needs, for instance. Does he need some sort of transportation where he's working, special equipment or supplies such as medicines, or a place for a growing church to meet? The more specific requests you have, the more your group can pray intelligently and rejoice when God answers your prayers.

Your meeting should conclude with prayer for the needs discussed that night. Some of the groups of which I'm aware also take up an offering to help with a specific need mentioned by a visiting missionary. One group has raised tens of thousands of dollars over a period of years, and some of the members have had the thrill of personally delivering supplies and equipment that their money bought.

I hope you will get involved in missions by making your home a missions center. Missions can be exciting as you reach out in prayer and concern to all parts of the world and see God use your prayers and other support to bring lost souls to a saving knowledge of Jesus Christ.

There's a fifth way you can be a sender of missionaries, and it's probably the one you expected to see first. I'm referring, of course, to giving financial support. I deliberately saved it until now because I wanted you to seriously consider first other ways in which you can advance the cause of world evangelization. I hope your eyes have been opened to some possibilities you hadn't thought of before, and that your own imagination has been stirred.

The fact remains, however, that God wants you to support the work of missions with the financial resources He has entrusted to you. Please understand that God doesn't need your money. He is the sovereign Lord, and whatever He wants done will get done whether you cooperate or not. His work will not grind to a halt if you don't give. Then why should you give?

First, you should give because you know God wants you to. If He is your Master and King, that should be reason enough. The Old Testament law required the people of Israel to tithe. In the New Testament, Jesus just assumed God's people would give, and He gave instructions for how to do it properly (in private, not seeking glory from others for how generous you are [see Matt. 6:1–4]). And Paul and the other apostles repeatedly commended and instructed the young churches for their support of them and of less-fortunate Christians in other cities.

Another reason you should give is that if you do it with the right attitude—cheerfully, out of gratitude to God—you'll feel good about it and God will be pleased. The happiest, most fulfilled people I know are those who give the most generously of themselves and their resources. They know the freedom of using money for good purposes rather than being slaves to material possessions. And it brings joy to the Father's heart when His children give cheerfully to His work. This is why Paul wrote, "So let each one give as he purposes in his heart, not grudgingly or of necessity; for God loves a cheerful giver" (2 Cor. 9:7).

A third reason to give is that God rewards those who do. Jesus said, "Give, and it will be given to you: good measure, pressed down, shaken together, and running over will be put into your bosom. For with the same measure that you use, it will be measured back to you" (Luke 6:38). And in Proverbs we see this wisdom: "The generous soul will be made rich, and he who waters will also be watered himself" (11:25).

Now, do these promises mean God will always reward us materially if we give financial gifts to churches, missionaries, or ministries, as some are teaching today? No, I don't believe so. Those who give out of a sincere desire to serve God will always have their basic needs met, I'm convinced, but God doesn't promise to make us rich in the things of this world. What He does give is far more valuable: joy, fulfillment, and purpose for living, plus heavenly rewards in the life to come.

Jesus told us, "do not lay up for yourselves treasures on earth, where moth and rust destroy and where thieves break in and steal; but lay up for yourselves treasures in heaven, where neither moth nor rust destroys and where thieves do not break in and steal. For where your treasure is, there your heart will be also" (Matt. 6:19–21).

The last sentence suggests a final reason why we should give. I believe God sees the way we use our money as a test of our love for Him. If we truly love Him and want to see His work of evangelism advanced, we'll be eager to give toward that cause. But if we're unwilling to give, then no matter what we *say*, our actions demonstrate our hearts are not in God's work. Whichever way we go, our use of money reveals what we love most.

I hope you're convinced to give financially to the work of missions. Now let me give you some guidelines for how to do it. First, while cash is the most obvious thing to give, it's certainly not the only way to give. Almost anything of value can be given— stocks, bonds, property, cars, supplies, and so on. You can also include a missions agency or evangelistic ministry in your will.

There are people at most such organizations who will be glad to explain how you can go about giving these kinds of gifts.

I would also suggest that you develop a giving plan in order to make your gifts most effective. By this I mean that you should give regularly, if possible, because the needs of any ministry are ongoing. Further, I recommend that you concentrate your giving to just a few ministries rather than trying to respond to every appeal you receive in the mail. Why?

First, as you probably know already if you give at all, once you give a gift to one ministry, you're likely to receive letters from many other ministries. Unless you're rich, you can't possibly give to everyone who makes a request. So choose those few for which God has given you a special burden, and trust Him to lay a burden for other ministries on the hearts of other Christians. He will, and their needs will be met for as long as they're a part of God's plan.

Second, if you concentrate on a few ministries, you can get to know them and their people well over a period of time. That way you'll be more abreast of what they're doing and what their needs are, and you'll feel that you're more a part of their work. That's good for both you and them.

Third—and I hate to have to say this—but there are unscrupulous people who will try to take your money under false pretenses. They will pose as legitimate ministries when they're really using donors' money to line their own pockets. If you concentrate your giving on a few ministries you know and can trust, you can more easily verify that your money has been put to good use.

Go for the Short Term

In the last chapter, I discussed the option of short-term missionary service for those who don't feel called to a lifelong overseas commitment. This is not something you can do without leaving home, but you can do it now. It is an additional way you can support the work of evangelism and missions. If you're convinced you're not meant to be a full-time missionary or evangelist, you should give serious consideration to a short-term mission experience at least once in your life. It's something you won't forget, and I promise it will change your view of the world and of missions work.

Although anyone who wants to participate in short-term missions can work out the details to do so in one way or another, there are two groups of people who are in an especially good position to take advantage of the many opportunities available.

The first of these is young people, such as college students. They have an abundance of energy and enthusiasm, they are full of curiosity about the world and its people, and they're relatively free of obligations that make it difficult for older people to get away for any length of time. They might go away for a summer between school terms. Those who attend a Christian college might even be able to go on a short-term mission project as part of their course work.

The second group with unusual opportunity to participate is that growing number who are retired. Like the young people, they may be free of many of the obligations that tied them down when they were still employed full time. Rather than thinking their usefulness is ended and wondering what to do with themselves, retired people could be entering the most exciting, fulfilling part of their lives!

In addition to being available, retired folks have wisdom and skills that the young have not yet acquired. If you're retired, I would urge you to think seriously about short-term (or even full-time) missions service. Investigate it carefully and pray about it. You would be surprised at just how useful you could be on the mission field.

You Can Do a Lot

There are many ways in which you can be involved in the work of evangelism, which is the challenging purpose God has given you. The Great Commission is a command that all of us who are God's children must obey, but how we go about it can take a multitude of forms. The ideas I've presented in this chapter are by no means all that are available. What's important is that you seek God's leading and then jump in with both feet and share the lasting joy of those who are co-laborers with the Lord in the most important work in the world.

---

1. Richard Foster, *Celebration of Discipline*, p. 31.
2. Sterling W. Huston, *The Billy Graham Crusade Handbook* (Minneapolis: World Wide, 1983), pp. 29–30.

13

ENTER INTO THE
JOY OF YOUR LORD

WE BEGAN THIS BOOK by looking briefly at Hank and Sam, two people whose lives are very similar outwardly, but very different within. And we saw that this difference is the result of a basic decision Hank made some time ago but that Sam has so far refused to make—to submit himself to be a servant of the living God.

Day by day, Hank is motivated by a love of God and a conviction that God loves him. It is out of that trust in God's goodness that Hank is glad to commit himself to his heavenly Father.

Hank has also learned that it's only by taking the risk of total commitment to God that we can know the full and lasting joy of fellowship with Him, of finding God faithful, of finding His love to be constant and unwavering, and of knowing by experience that His promises are true.

Do you want lasting joy and satisfaction in your life? Then learn what Hank has learned, and do what he's done. "The secret of having joy," said Manford Gutzke, "is to give everything over to the Lord; and by the same sign the really sad and tragic secret of no joy is no sacrifice. Sometimes people say, 'I think that one thing the church today lacks is joy.' That is true. Do you know why? Because the people of the church haven't given enough of themselves. It hasn't cost enough."[1] The secret of lasting joy, then, is to be a servant of the living God.

Unlike Hank, Sam is motivated in the good things he does by a fear and mistrust of God. Unlike a true servant of the Lord who serves as a loving response to the love of his Master, Sam does what he does only because he's afraid of what God will do to him if he doesn't. Not surprisingly, then, his life isn't characterized by joy.

Now, Sam *is* born again by faith in the atoning work of Jesus Christ, but he labors under a faulty view of God. Consequently, he's also not at all convinced that committing himself fully to God's service would be anything but drudgery. Unfortunately, a lot of people—including many Christians—share that opinion with Sam. As Gutzke points out, "It is a common feeling that living a surrendered life as a Christian in humble obedience to God must be very dull and unrewarding. . . . No matter how the public may feel . . . this is simply not true. . . . It must be admitted that the joy of living in Christ is different from the joys of the flesh. That is true, but the Christian joy is more real and far more satisfying."[2]

Sam will never really believe what Dr. Gutzke said and act on it until he comes to better understand the love of God, which I hope this book has helped you to do. As Richard Foster said wisely, "Service that is duty-motivated breathes death. [But] service that flows out of our inward person is life, and joy and peace."[3] It's as if God were in a great room showering His love on all His servants, but the Sams of the world are outside, peeking through a crack in the door at what God offers, afraid to swing it open wide and walk into the Father's embrace. Are you a Sam?

Remember, because God is sovereign, His work will get done and His purposes will be accomplished whether you commit yourself to His service or not. But you'll be the loser if you don't because you'll miss the opportunity to be a part of what He's doing, and you'll never experience the joy of full fellowship with the Lord who loves you so.

What It Means to Be a God-Called Servant

In the four sections of this book, we've seen what it means to be a servant of God. It means first that God clearly calls *all* who are His children by faith to a life of service, which is only right because He redeemed us at the price of the blood of His Son, the Lord Jesus Christ.

Further, while He calls us all to serve, He calls us uniquely as individuals. Thus, the priorities and ministries He gives you will probably be different from mine, and we make a serious mistake if we expect all God's servants to look and act and minister like ourselves.

We must take care, too, to minister in His strength, not our own. If we try to do it by ourselves, we'll surely fail. Our own sinful natures, Satan, or the opposition even of other Christians will do us in. But when we rely on His strength, we can overcome obstacles and give Him the glory He deserves.

Second, we saw that God wants His servants to live clean, holy lives. We looked at the importance of what we allow into our minds and what we let them dwell on. If we put garbage into our minds, garbage will spill out of our mouths and our lives. God also gives us powerful resources to help us pursue holiness, including the indwelling Holy Spirit, the Bible, prayer, Christian fellowship, and a free will with which we can purpose in our hearts, as Daniel and his friends did, to stay clean in the face of temptation.

No matter how much we want to please the Lord by living holy lives, however, we'll all fail from time to time. There's no perfection this side of heaven. But when we fail, we have the marvelous reassurance that God still loves us and will never turn us away if we come back to Him with repentant hearts. Indeed, while we don't want to fail and it usually causes us and others much pain, God can use those experiences to make us even better servants in the future as we learn from our mistakes and gain compassion for others who fail.

Third, God calls His servants to proclaim a courageous message. He wants us to speak boldly on His behalf. Speaking for Him gives us both great freedom and a large responsibility, whether we are witnessing to our neighbor or trying to get people to hear us as we talk about one of the important issues of today such as the deity of Jesus Christ or abortion. We need to be careful in our enthusiasm, however, to realize that God has not called all Christians to speak about the same issues with the same intensity.

Given the fact that many Christians carry around spiritual "cookie cutters," trying to fit others into their mold, the important little word "no" must also be a part of our courageous message. We simply can't be and do all God wants us to be and do if we allow others to set our priorities and control our time.

Fourth, God gives us a challenging purpose, the greatest purpose in the world—that of being involved in reaching out to people everywhere with the good news of the gospel of Jesus Christ. God may be calling you to serve Him in this way as a full-time vocation.

Years ago, when I was in Korea during the great crusade Billy Graham had in Seoul where he preached to more than one million people at one time, it was my privilege to preach at Inchon. While I was riding there with my interpreter, I learned that Inchon was the place where General MacArthur had landed. But more important than that, Inchon was where the first missionaries to Korea were martyred. When those Presbyterian missionaries proclaimed the gospel of Jesus Christ, they were killed.

As I rode to Inchon, I realized that I would be preaching on the very spot where those wonderful men and women of God had shed their blood. The thought overwhelmed me. I felt I had an obligation not only to the Lord Jesus Christ, but to those martyred missionaries as well. I opened my heart and as I preached I asked God to help me preach as I had never done before. We had a tremendous response that Sunday afternoon.

Those martyred missionaries lived with a challenging purpose. And they left that purpose as a legacy to those who followed them—including me.

But even if God has not called you to the vocation of a missionary or evangelist, there are many ways in which you can be a part of this effort, both in the local church and on your own. Not the least of these is to pray faithfully, regularly, and intelligently for those who are on the front lines of evangelistic work. For while they are on the front lines, God blesses their work through the intercession of His praying servants.

The Promise of Reward

By now, I hope I've given you sufficient understanding and motivation to offer yourself as a willing servant to the Lord Who loves you. I trust it makes sense to you when I say that such a life is the most fulfilling and joy-filled way to live. I have found it to be so even though it was difficult for me to put aside my own ambitions. Twenty-five years ago, I gave up my own evangelistic team and took a position with Billy Graham.

I had known Billy since we were both boys. I was at a crusade with him, and about two o'clock one morning he asked me to work for him. I said, "Billy, I know what I am supposed to do [I wanted to lead my own evangelistic team], and let's not talk anymore about my joining you."

He said, "T. W., I need someone to help me. I need someone who knows me and who knows my family. I need someone who is an evangelist himself. I believe this would be a great ministry for you."

"Billy," I said, "this is not for me."

"T. W., I want to ask you one question. Are you more interested in the number of times you can speak or in the most good you can do for almighty God?"

"Oh, that's beside the point," I said.

Billy then asked me if I would pray about it.

"I don't need to pray about it. I know what I'm supposed to do."

"Do you mean there is something in your life you cannot pray about?" Billy asked me.

I knew the answer, and I knew he was right. I tossed and I turned and I couldn't sleep that night. The next morning I called my wife and told her of Billy Graham's challenge to me. "Darling," she said, "I have one bit of advice to give you: Make sure you are in God's will. If you are not in His will, you will be miserable. And if you are miserable, we will both be miserable."

After I tossed and turned and after I prayed and sought God's will, it seemed that God was telling me to accept Billy's offer. I did, and I have never regretted it. But I had to give up my own ambitions and become a servant not only of Jesus Christ, but also of Billy Graham.

Being a servant of Jesus Christ and of Billy Graham doesn't lessen the importance of the ways in which God uses me. It's like playing in a great orchestra. We can't all play first chair or be the soloist, but every instrument in the orchestra is important. We on the Billy Graham team have worked together trying to honor the Lord Jesus Christ who has called all of us to be His servants. I have thoroughly enjoyed it.

I hope you also will realize that being God's servant is the most fulfilling and joy-filled way to live. It has been for me. But just in case that's not enough, there's more. For in addition to everything else, God offers rewards in heaven to His faithful servants.

The apostle Paul spoke of these rewards in terms of a crown: "Do you not know that those who run in a race all run, but one receives the prize? Run in such a way that you may obtain it. And everyone who competes for the prize is temperate in all things. Now they do it to obtain a perishable crown, but we for an imperishable crown" (1 Cor. 9:24–25).

Just what form these crowns might take we do not know. We can be sure, however, that what God promises, He will give, and it will be far better than anything we can imagine now. And the best reward we could possibly receive will be to pass through heaven's gates and hear our Father God say, "Well done, good and faithful servant. . . . Enter into the joy of your Lord" (Matt. 25:21). Now *that's* lasting joy! My prayer for you is that God will be pleased to give you such a greeting in that day.

---

1. Manford George Gutzke, *Born to Serve*, p. 131.
2. Ibid., pp. 104–5.
3. Richard Foster, *Celebration of Discipline*, p. 122.

"The Key to Lasting Joy is a good book. No, it is a *superb* book. The chapter entitled "No Cookie Cutters, Please" is alone worth the price of the book. T. W. Wilson has done church members everywhere a magnificent service in the penning of this monograph."

—Dr. W. A. Criswell
Pastor, First Baptist
Church of Dallas

"T. W. Wilson has written a book which is, like him, inspiring, challenging, and full of integrity."

—Cal Thomas
Columnist, Los Angeles
Times Syndicate

". . . a much needed book that will be of tremendous help and blessing. . . . This book brings us back to the basics."

—Dr. Cliff Barrows
Greenville, South Carolina

"T. W. has woven an heirloom "comforter" to warm our spirits, skillfully threading together Scriptures, common sense, and his characteristic sensitivity for the peril and the potential of being human."

—Dr. Mel Lorentzen
The Billy Graham Center
Wheaton College

"In *The Key to Lasting Joy,* we find questions we are asking and the answers we are seeking. This book is truly 'down to earth,' but it also reaches into heaven."

—Dr. Charles Allen
Pastor Emeritus, First United
Methodist Church of Houston

"Dr. Wilson is one of the great Christian statesmen of our time. Reading this book is a genuine treat. . . ."

—Dr. Ben Armstrong
Executive Director
National Religious Broadcasters

"Why was not *The Key to Lasting Joy* written twenty years ago? Think of all the grief it could have saved!"

—Marabel Morgan
Author, President
The Total Woman

"*The Key to Lasting Joy* will be a blessing to all who read it."

—Dr. Allan C. Emery, Jr.
President, The Billy Graham
Evangelistic Association

"Wilson's book is gentle, kind, embracing, like the man himself, accepting the many modes of Christian service and individual ways . . . down-to-earth, gracious, and practical."

—George W. Cornell
Religion Writer
Associated Press

"His honesty and insight will inspire and inform all who desire to know how to love Christ more, serve Him better . . . and have fun while doing it."

—Dr. Stephen Brown
Pastor, Key Biscayne
Presbyterian Church

"I highly recommend this book to all who are seeking the will of God in the light of the Word of God."

—Dr. Grady Wilson
Vice-President, The Billy Graham
Evangelistic Association

"Anyone can have fleeting moments of pleasure and happiness. But in these chapters, T. W. Wilson offers the key to *lasting* joy."

—Dr. Roger C. Palms
Editor, *Decision* Magazine

"T. W. Wilson has gone to the heart of discipleship and what it entails. . . . New Christians and veterans alike will find both challenge and help to meet that challenge as Christ's lordship is winsomely presented in these chapters."

—Dr. David Allan Hubbard
President, Fuller Theological
Seminary

". . . a fresh portrayal of familiar biblical truths with contemporary illustration and application . . . practical help in regaining the proper perspective on real values in this life and the next."

—Dr. Harper Shannon
Director of Evangelism
Alabama Baptist State Convention

"In this encouraging book, Dr. Wilson shares with us practical, applicable, spiritual, and sensible counsel and advice for those of us who want to enjoy the biblical promise of the 'joy of the Lord.' "

—Dr. Ted W. Engstrom
President, World Vision

". . . a veteran handing on to a new generation the biblical truths and common wisdom that have lasting value."

—Dr. John A. Huffman
Senior Minister, St. Andrews
Presbyterian Church in Newport

". . . vintage T. W. Wilson! Great wisdom from the perspective of a world evangelist. . . . Hearts will be warmed and stirred."

—Dr. Denton Lotz
Director of Evangelism
Baptist World Alliance

"In a day characterized by numerous options to evangelical Christianity, a book born out of the Word of God and nurtured by rich experience in many lands demonstrates the superiority of the faith of our Lord."

—Dr. Paige Patterson
President, The Criswell College

"T.W., a warm servant of Christ, speaks with a joy of verities lived. The basic truths of this book apply to us all."

—Harold I. Myra
President, *Christianity Today*

"No one is better qualified to describe the elements of true joy than T. W. Wilson. In this book he clearly tells us why there is so little in our lives and how we can get it. Fill your life with true happiness. Read *The Key to Lasting Joy.*

—Dr. Robert H. Schuller
Senior Minister
Crystal Cathedral

"This book is truly a handbook for Christians . . . It will change your life and enhance your Christian awareness."

—Tom Landry
Head Coach
Dallas Cowboys